THE
LITTLE GIANT® BOOK OF
TRAVEL FUN

THE
LITTLE GIANT® BOOK OF
TRAVEL FUN

Sheila Anne Barry
Illustrated by Jeff Sinclair

Sterling Publishing Co., Inc.
New York

Library of Congress Cataloging-in-Publication Data Available

10 9 8 7 6 5 4 3

Published by Sterling Publishing Company, Inc.
387 Park Avenue South, New York, N.Y. 10016
Additional text and illustrations © 2001 by Sheila Anne Barry
One section of this book was previously published under the
title "World's Best Travel Games © 1983 by Sheila Anne Barry
The lateral thinking puzzles in the book have been excerpted
from "Challenging Lateral Thinking Puzzles" © 1992 by
Paul Sloane and Des MacHale and "Great Lateral Thinking
Puzzles" © 1994 by Paul Sloane and Des MacHale
Distributed in Canada by Sterling Publishing
c/o Canadian Manda Group, One Atlantic Avenue, Suite 105
Toronto, Ontario, Canada M6K 3E7
Distributed in Great Britain and Europe by Chris Lloyd
463 Ashley Road, Parkstone, Poole, Dorset,
BH14 0AX, England
Distributed in Australia by Capricorn Link (Australia) Pty Ltd.
P.O. Box 6651, Baulkham Hills, Business Centre, NSW 2153,
Australia

Manufactured in Canada
All rights reserved

Sterling ISBN 0-8069-3690-8

To my mother
—one of the world's best travelers—
who taught me what fun it can be to go
places and play games.

Contents

Odd Animals • The Elder Twin • Hand in Glove • Clues

10. Quizzes   311

What Did They Have in Common? • Animated Film Quiz #1 • Animated Film Quiz #2 • Weather Quiz • Festivals and Holidays Quiz

BEFORE YOU BEGIN

If it's true that half the fun of going places is getting there, then it's certainly important to enjoy the time you spend on the plane or train, in the car or the bus, walking or waiting.

Sometimes it's easy to enjoy all of it, because there are interesting people to look at, because the atmosphere is different and exciting, or because there's so much new going on around you.

At other times it's not so easy. Driving on expressways, thruways, turnpikes, freeways—whatever you call them—can be pretty boring. And so is jetting through the blue-and-white skies. That's where these games come in.

Some of them just help you open your eyes to what is actually going on around you (such as the car games starting on page 47). Some of them make you think. Some are hilarious. All of them are fun.

Most of the games can be played anywhere, but if you're not sure, look at the icon at the top of the page, which will show you where you can use it:

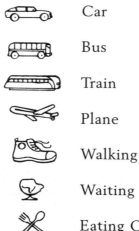

Car

Bus

Train

Plane

Walking

Waiting

Eating Out

and you'll be able to tell straight off whether it's a game that's right for you at that moment. You'll also see at a glance if you can play it alone or with one other person or more.

So—now to the games! Have a great trip!

1 The Great Guessing Games

Most of the games in this section are famous, and it's no wonder, because they get more interesting the more you play them.

They all work pretty much the same way. One of the players thinks of a subject and the others guess what it is.

But the subject can be practically anything—and the possibilities are endless! Once the players realize how wide-open their choices are, and get used to the tricks and shortcuts and strategies of guessing, the games can become challenging beyond belief.

I SPY

Players: 2 or more
Equipment: None
Preparation: None

The least complex of all the guessing games, this is a good quickie for playing when you don't have much time. It calls for no moving about, no great concentration, and the only requirement is that you stay in one place long enough to complete a round of the game.

First you choose a subject, which can be anything that is in full view of all the players. Then you reveal one thing about the subject. You could say, "I see something red," or "I see something soft," or "I see something metal." But you don't say anything else about it.

The other player or players then start to guess what your subject is. Instead of answering just "yes" or "no," you answer according to how close they come—in space—to the subject.

For example, let's say you're on a plane and it's just before dinner. Your subject is the brown tie of the steward who is moving up and down the aisle, serving meals.

YOU: I see something brown.
CHARLIE: Is it your sweater?

YOU (*glancing at the steward, who is all the way in the front of the plane unloading trays*): No, you're cold, very cold.

CHARLIE (*looking toward the front of the plane at a passenger close to the steward*): Is it that blond guy's leather jacket?

YOU (*answering slowly, as the steward makes his way down the aisle toward you*): No, you're lukewarm. Actually, you're cold....Yes, you're getting colder by the minute.

CHARLIE (*baffled*): What do you mean by *that*?

BARBARA (*in the aisle seat, taking a tray from the steward and grinning—she thinks she knows*): Is it the steward's big brown eyes?

YOU: No, but you're blazing hot.

Well, you get the idea. Charlie or Barbara will probably guess that your subject has something to do with the steward, and the round will soon be over. Just in time, or the food on those trays would get cold. Sometimes you *need* a short game.

NAME THAT TUNE

Players: 2 or more
Equipment: None
Preparation: None

Here's a classic game that you can play just about anywhere—indoors or out, riding, walking, or sitting—and it's also quick and easy. All you need is something to tap with and something to tap against. Your knuckles or fingernail will do for the tapper. A book, tabletop, dashboard, or watch crystal will do for the tappee. Or you could just clap.

First you tap out the rhythm of a song. Then your opponents need to guess what the song is. Start with simple, well-known tunes with a strong, distinctive rhythm, like "Hail, Hail the Gang's All Here" or "Jingle Bells." As you get used to hearing rhythm separate from melody, you'll find that you can recognize tunes more easily.

At the beginning, it's a good idea to take turns tapping out the songs. After you play for a while you can start following the standard rules:

One player taps out a tune. The player who guesses it becomes the tapper. If no one guesses the tune correctly, the original tapper gets another turn and taps out a new tune.

If just two of you are playing, take turns tapping, but a wrong guess gets you a point. Five points and you lose.

TWENTY QUESTIONS

Players: 2 or more
Equipment: None
Preparation: None

"Twenty Questions" is a far better game than most people realize, or it can be if you use imagination when you choose your subject. It is one of the simplest guessing games, and people of all ages can play it.

One person thinks of a person, place, or thing and announces to the group whether it is animal, vegetable, or mineral.

Animal is anything in the animal kingdom from a human being to a sponge, but it could also be anything made from an animal skin (like a leather wallet) or it could be part of an animal, like the jaws of the great white shark or a strip of bacon. It could also be groups of people, like all the people who live in Seattle or all the people who go out on

21

blind dates. It could be supernatural creatures, like Batman or the Frankenstein monster, or nursery-rhyme characters like Mary, Mary Quite Contrary. It could also be part of a fictional person, like Dracula's tooth.

Vegetable is anything that grows on trees or in the ground. It could be something made from things that grow, like paper or a book, like spaghetti or perfume. It could also be penicillin (made from bread mold), a rubber hot-water bottle or skis or some specific thing, like the pines of Rome, the poison apple the wicked Queen prepared for Snow White, or all the French fries McDonald's serves in a year.

23

It could be Harry Potter's broom

Mineral is just about everything else—rocks and stones, but also water, salt, glass, plastic, or the Emerald City of Oz.

Back to the game: One player announces the classification of the subject and then the guessers get 20 questions in which to find out what it is. The questions must be ones that can be answered yes, no, partly, or sometimes. The player who guesses what it is becomes the next player to select the subject.

Think out your questions carefully so that you can eliminate many possibilities each time.

Questions that are too specific too soon can be wasted. If you think you know the answer and are not too near the 20th question, continue to pin it down with general questions before you ask a direct one.

Here is a sample game. The subject is the Three Bears—animal.

1. Is it human? No.
2. Is it 4-legged? Yes.
3. Is this a carnivorous animal? No.
4. Is it bigger than a breadbox? (Few people have breadboxes these days, but this is a classic question.) Yes.
5. Is it bigger than I am? Partly. (The idea being that Pappa and Momma Bear are bigger, but Baby Bear isn't.)
6. Is more than one animal involved? Yes.
7. Are they land animals? Yes.
8. Are they dangerous? Yes.
9. Are they found in North America? Yes.
10. Are they hairy? Yes.
11. Are they bears? Yes.
12. Are they bears who attacked people? No.

13. Are these bears fictional? Yes.
14. Are there more than three of them? No.
15. Are they the Three Bears? Yes.

You don't have to stick with individual people or things as subjects. As you get skillful at this game, you may want to go really far out, with things like:

All the women in the world who are going to have twins this year

All the hockey players in Canada

The heel of Cinderella's glass slipper

The tears on the faces of the girls Georgie Porgie kissed.

27

A few notes about strategy: If you find your friends often pick famous people as subjects, you might want to ask opening questions that identify them right away. When "Twenty Questions" was played on the radio many decades ago, the players used to ask, "Is this a living American male?" as a shortcut question, and it usually saved them lots of time. But whatever shortcut questions you develop will depend on your group. If you find that most of the subjects are film stars, you might want to ask, "Is this a living person in the entertainment world?"

Of course, once people get used to your asking that kind of question, they'll start avoiding that categoy and reach farther afield for subjects. But that will only make the game more interesting.

WHO ARE YOU?

Players: 2 or more
Equipment: None
Preparation: None

This is a simpler variation on "Twenty Questions," but it has a charm of its own. One of the players actually "becomes" the subject, and the others ask questions directly. Let's say that you have decided to be Clark Kent (Superman), and the game begins:

HARVEY: What is your profession?
YOU: I'm in journalism.
SANDY: Is that what made you famous?
YOU: Not really. I guess it was my work in law enforcement.
CASSIE: Are you married?
YOU: No.
CASSIE: In love?
YOU: Absolutely.

SANDY: What do you do for fun?

YOU: I don't have much time for fun, actually.

HARVEY: What keeps you so busy?

YOU: Well, I take my responsibilities very seriously, and a lot of people depend on me.

CASSIE: Are you American?

YOU: Yes, but I wasn't born in the States.

And so on. You can have some fun with the answers you give. While they have to be truthful, they don't have to be complete!

You're not limited to 20 questions in this game. The players just keep asking questions until they figure out who you are or give up. If they give up, you get to go again. The one who guesses your identify becomes the next mystery character.

This game can get more complex, too. Let's say that you're all the people who ever played hookey from school.

HARVEY: What is your profession?

YOU: I'm a student.

SANDY: What are you most famous for?

YOU: Well, I'm not exactly proud of that.

HARVEY: How so?

YOU: It's for doing something I wasn't supposed to do.

CASSIE: Something illegal?

YOU: Sort of.

SANDY: Did you profit from doing it?

YOU: I'm afraid not, but I thought I did at the time.

Sooner of later the others will realize that the key is the thing you did and when you did it, and that there is more than one of you.

GRANDMA IS STRANGE

Players: 2 or more
Equipment: None
Preparation: None

In this game, each player takes turns having a strange grandmother. The first player—say, Laurie—starts out:

"My grandma is very strange. She loves tennis, but she hates games."

Laurie's statement is based on a secret combination that she has thought up.

The next player asks a question, testing: "Does she like carrots?"

"Yes," says Laurie, and gives them another clue, "but she hates peas."

"Does she like dogs?"

"No, but she's crazy about raccoons."

Laurie's secret combination is that her grandmother likes anything that has a double letter in it, like buttons but not bows, zoos

but not animals, pepper but not salt.

As players discover Laurie's grandmother's secret, they join her in giving clues to the other players.

You can go on for hours with this game. The last player to catch on to the secret is the next one to have a strange grandmother.

That's the usual way to play this game, and once you discover the formula, the game is over.

But actually, this is where the fun begins.

Grandma can be strange in different ways: she can hate anything that has a certain letter in it. Or anything that grows (watch out, that's a tricky one—*many* things grow). Or anything with two syllables (she hates flying but she loves jets). Or anything with two legs. Or four-letter words. Or anything that doesn't smell.

COFFEEPOT

Players: 2–12
Equipment: None
Preparation: None

In this game "coffeepot" becomes a verb—a verb that you (or your group) think up secretly. Your opponent must guess what it is by asking a series of questions. In each question the word "coffeepot" is used for the hidden verb, and the questions must be answerable by yes and no.

Suppose you are on the guessing end of the game. You might start with, "Do people coffeepot?"

"Do I coffeepot?"

"Do you coffeepot?"

"Do all human beings coffeepot?"

If the answer to the last question is no, you will need to narrow down the field and find out if only boys coffeepot, or perhaps only

old people do it, or only married women, etc. If you don't seem to be getting any results, try another tack.

"Do you need any tools to coffeepot?"

"Do you coffeepot only in certain places or at certain times of the year or of the day?"

"Do animals coffeepot?"

"Is coffeepotting fun?" Difficult? Part of a job? A natural function?

After you have narrowed down the field and think you are pretty sure you know what "coffeepot" is, you get three guesses. It's a good idea, though, to ask as many specific questions as possible before you guess.

Suppose you've found out that young people coffeepot but not small children, that you coffeepot outdoors, that you don't coffeepot in the dark, that you coffeepot in warm weather, that you use a long pole to coffeepot, that neither you nor your opponent coffeepot yourselves, and that coffeepotting takes skill, strength, and practice. You think the answer may be "to pole vault."

Then you might check to make sure by asking, "Does anyone ever coffeepot at the Olympics?" If the answer is yes, you know that you're right.

If you're playing Coffeepot in a place where one person can leave the room, the others should decide what Coffeepot is. Then the guesser comes back in and asks each player one or more questions. When the guesser gets the answer, he or she selects the next one to guess.

If you're in close quarters in a car or in a restaurant, say, and more than two want to play, let one person select the Coffeepot word, while the others ask the questions.

BOTTICELLI

Players: 2–10
Equipment: None
Preparation: None

Botticelli (pronounced Botta-CHELLY) is one of the great guessing games, and it can be played by anyone from eight up. The more knowledgeable the group, the more fun.

One player thinks of a person, real or fictional, living or dead, and tells the group only the first letter of the person's last name. The others have to guess who it is, but they are only allowed to guess if they already have someone in mind. For instance, let's say the subject is Botticelli, the Italian artist. Here is part of a game.

MARK: I am a famous person whose name begins with B.

42

HAL: Are you a famous composer? *(He is thinking of Beethoven.)*

MARK: No, I am not Bach.

LIZ: Are you a character from the comics?

MARK: No, I am not Charlie Brown.

LAEL: Are you a comedy writer?

MARK: No, I am not Mel Brooks.

JIM: Are you an actor?

MARK: No I am not George Burns.

HAL *(still trying for Beethoven, but he can't ask the same question the same way twice)*: Are you a composer who went deaf?

MARK: No, I am not Beethoven.

(Hal revealed too much. It would have been better if he had known some obscure fact about Beethoven that would disguise his idea so that Mark would not have thought of Beethoven so easily.)

LIZ: Are you a U.S. President?

MARK *(stumped)*: I challenge you.

LIZ: Buchanan!

(Liz, having stumped Mark, gets a leading question, which will help the group find out who Mark is. The leading question must be one

that can be answered yes or no.)

LIZ: Are you male?

MARK *(must answer a leading question truthfully)*: Yes.

LAEL: Are you a famous painter? *(She is thinking of Botticelli.)*

MARK: Yes, but I am not Bosch.

(Mark had to admit that Lael had guessed the right profession. But he didn't have to admit that he was Botticelli as long as he could think of another painter beginning with B.)

JIM: Are you a famous general?

MARK *(stumped again)*: I challenge you.

JIM: Napoleon Bonaparte! I get a leading question. Are you alive?

MARK: No.

BILL: Are you a famous baseball player?

MARK: No, I am not Yogi Berra.

LIZ: Are you a pioneer?

MARK: No, I am not Daniel Boone.

LAEL *(still trying for Botticelli)*: Are you a famous Italian artist?

MARK: Yes, but not Michelangelo Buonarroti.

(Now Lael is stuck. She doesn't know any more facts about Botticelli that she can use to ask another question. She cannot repeat her last question without changing it a little. She has to wait for a chance at a leading question before she can pinpoint the person. If she gets to stump Mark again, before anyone else does, she can ask the leading question "Are you Botticelli?" and then she will be the next one to think of a person.)

BOTTICELLI FOR EXPERTS

For a much more difficult game, the players restrict their questions each time they get information through a leading question.

For example, once the players know that the subject is male, they can ask questions about only male subjects. Once they know, from a leading question, that the person is dead, they can ask questions only about dead people. Don't try this unless you're really a super-Botticelli player or have tremendous stores of historical and cultural information.

2 On the Road

You can play many of the games in other sections when you're in the car or on a bus, but some games have been invented especially for motor trips. They don't get you involved in words or ideas (at least, most of them don't), but they're focused primarily on the road, the other cars, the license plates, the countryside, the signs.

THE TRAFFIC GAME

Players: 2
Equipment: None
Preparation: None

You're waiting for something—for a bus, for a taxi, for someone to come back to the car, for a third friend to arrive—whatever—and you're doing it near a two-way street or highway. Perfect—you can play the Traffic Game.

The rules couldn't be simpler. You score one point for every car that passes from the right. Your friend scores one for every car that passes from the left. When your wait is over (the bus comes, the driver gets back, your friend arrives), the one with the most points wins.

COLLECTING ALL CARS

Players: 2 or more
Equipment: Paper and pencil (optional)
Preparation: None

The object of the game is to "collect" as many cars as you can. You collect a car by "owning" the place it comes from—or some other fact you can get from the license plate. If you're in the U.S. or Australia, for example, you own the state. And you get to own a state by being the first person to spot a car from that state.

Let's say you're in Connecticut and you've just started out on your trip. Cars from Connecticut, New York, and New Jersey are automatically out of the game, because there are just too many of them. But you're the first to spot a car from Louisiana.

"Louisiana!" you shout. "I own Louisiana!"

And for the rest of the game, any time you

see a car from Louisiana, you add it to your score—one point per car.

If you're walking or driving in Canada, you can play the game by owning the different provinces (*not* the one you're in). If you're traveling in the U.K., you can play it by owning one of the letters or digits on the marker (the license plate). All cars with a 6 on the marker, for instance, could be owned, and so could all cars with an L or all cars with a combination of 6 and M.

One of the passengers or walkers can keep tabs on who owns which state, province, digit, letter, or combination, in case there's a dispute, but usually everyone remembers. You can decide ahead of time how long you want to play—or you can play until you arrive at your destination. The one with the most points wins.

CAR MAKES

Players: 2 or more
Equipment: Paper and pencil (optional)
Preparation: None

How would you like to own all the cars on the road?

Divide up the car manufacturers listed on the next page among the players. Or you can just each take a few of them, 3 or 4 or 5. Whatever you do, though, make sure that each player has at least one of the most popular makes—Toyota, Honda, Ford, etc.

Decide how long you will play for—10 minutes, 15, or half an hour. Then, any time you see a car that belongs to you, you score a point. The one with the most points, wins.

Toyota	BMW
Honda	Cadillac
Ford	Geo
Chevrolet	Isuzu
Chrysler	Jeep
Mitsubishi	Mercedes Benz
Dodge	Lincoln/Mercury
Oldsmobile	Saturn
Buick	Nissan
Pontiac	Saab
Subaru	Volkswagen
Plymouth	Ferrari
Mazda	Jaguar
Volvo	Lexus
Hyundai	Peugeot
Daewood	Porsche
Acura	Rolls-Royce
Audi	Alfa Romeo

55

LICENSE PLATE NUMBERS

Players: 1 or more
Equipment: A watch (optional)
Preparation: None

This is a good game to play in heavy traffic, especially when a lot of cars are passing you. The object is to find numbers from 1 to 20 on the license plates you see along the road. The rule is that you can score only one number at a time in sequence.

For example, let's say the first license plate you see is NSW5. You can't score any points because the only number you can use at this point in the game is a 1. If a car came along with the license plate 1M237, for instance, you'd be able to score the number 1, and then you'd need to start looking for a license plate with a 2 in it. You can't score the 2 and 3 from the same plate, because only one number can be scored from any one license plate.

When you get into double numbers—from 10 to 20—the two digits you need must come side by side. S7FU208, for example would give you 20, but S7FU028 would not.

If you're playing alone, take a look at your watch before you start and see how long it takes you to locate all 20 numbers. Then you can play against your best time.

If you're playing with more than one person, the first one to spot the needed number is the one who gets to score, and each player works on his or her own count. So one person can be looking for an 18 while the other is searching for an 8.

This game can get exciting for the players. But don't ask the driver to play! That could get hair-raising!

THE FAST GAME

Use the same rules as before, but this time allow more than one number to score from any license plate. For example, the license plate 123M7 would give you 1 and 2 and 3, and if any players were up to 12 in their lists, they could claim that number from the same license plate.

LICENSE PLATE LETTERS

This game is played the same way, but instead of numbers from 1 to 20, you search for the letters A to Z.

LICENSE PLATE WORDS

Players: 1 or more
Equipment: None
Preparation: None

This license-plate game goes one step further than finding numbers or letters. Here the players select words, phrases, or even sentences that they are going to try to spell out from license plates.

In any one round, every player needs to pick a word or phrase with exactly the same number of letters. The length depends on how long you want the game to last. Anywhere from six to ten letters makes a good game. Starting with six letters, for example, you could use:

BE COOL	HOT DOG
BIG MAC	UPBEAT
BY JOVE	OLD HAT

CATNIP   SLY FOX
GO HOME   GHOSTS

or anything else with six letters. After each
player picks a word, phrase, or sentence, you
race to see who can spell it out first from the
letters on the license plates of passing cars.
You can take a letter form anywhere in the
license plate. So A875BQ and B167WA and

CAT95 would all give you an A, but you can't take a letter from a license plate if someone else claimed the letter first.

If Barry's phrase is COLD CASH, for instance, he can take the C from CAT95 if he claims it first, and no one else can use it. But Julia, if her phrase is AWAY WE GO, can take the A from the same license plate, and another player can take the T.

You need to collect all the letters in the right order. So if MAKE MY DAY is your phrase, you need to find an M first, then an A, then a K and so on. Decide beforehand whether one player may take two or more letters from the same license plate. For example, could a player with the word CATNIP take the CAT from the CAT95 license plate? It's up to you—but if you allow it, the game goes faster.

If you're playing alone, as in the other license-plate games, you can time yourself and play against your best score.

Here are a few more ideas for words and phrases:

With 7 letters:

ALL OF ME
BAD SHOT
BIG BIRD
DOWN BOY
DRACULA
GOOD DOG
HALFWIT
OLD MAID
RAT FINK

With 8 letters:

AWAY WE GO
CALM DOWN
CRAZY MAN
GO TO JAIL
I LOVE YOU
LUCKY DAY
NAPOLEON
STARSHIP

With 9 letters:

BOARDWALK
BROAD JUMP
GOING NUTS
HAPPY DAYS
MAKE MY DAY
PARK PLACE
ROCKY ROAD
SAY CHEESE

With 10 letters:

ADAM AND EVE
CINDERELLA
DONALD DUCK
FLINTSTONE
GO FOR BROKE
HAVE A HAPPY
NEW ENGLAND
RUB A DUB DUB

NUMBER OF THE DAY

Players: 1 or more
Equipment: A watch (optional)
Preparation: None

The players decide on an order of play—clock-wise or counterclockwise—in the car or bus or whatever. And then they pick a number: let's say number 5.

The first car to pass belongs to Tom, the first player. The license plate is 867EN. No 5s. Tom's turn is over.

The second player, Dick, gets the next car to pass: 151N81. He scores one point for the 5.

Now it's Harry's turn. The next car to come along has the license plate 55CN25. Harry gets three points, one for each of the 5s.

And it's Tom's turn again.

First player to get 25 points wins. If you want a short game, set a lower number.

If you want to play the game alone, time yourself to see how long it takes you to get to your goal number. Then play against your own best time.

CAR OF YOUR CHOICE

Players: 2 or more
Equipment: A watch
Preparation: None

Each player chooses a make of car—Toyota, Ford, Volkswagen, whatever. Over a set period of time, say 15 minutes, each one tries to spot as many models from that car maker as possible. When the time is up, the player who spotted the most cars from his or her manufacturer is the winner.

ALPHABET ON ROAD AND TRACK

Players: 2 or more
Equipment: Paper and pencil for each player
    or team
Preparation: None

Contestants may be two individuals or two
teams. Each one looks for the first signs they
can find—a billboard or a road sign—that
contains an A, such as "Downtown Augusta
turn right."

The player (or the team) that sees it first
writes it down and circles the A.

Then they try to find a road sign containing
a B. The first player (or team) to complete
the alphabet wins. If you spot a phrase
containing two desired letters *in order*, such
as the D and e in Dover, you may copy that
word and circle both letters.

71

EAGLE EYE

Players: 2 or more
Equipment: A list you draw up ahead of time
Preparation: See below.

To begin the game, draw up a list of the objects you are likely to see as you drive along, taking into consideration the kind of road you're on and the part of the country you're in. For example, you would assign a higher point value to an Eskimo if you happen to be in Brazil than you would while driving through Alaska. The player who sights the object first gets the points, and every time the same sort of object is sighted again, you can score it again.

Winner is the player who gets the highest score in a given period of time, usually half an hour.

73

Here is a sample scale of points:

Rest stop	1
Horses (one or more)	2
Red light	1
Railroad crossing	2
Freight train	2
Bus	1
Police car	1
Tow truck	2
Convertible	1
Cemetery	1
Church	2
Red barn	1
Farmer in field	2
Farmer in field with plow	4
Cyclist	3
Sheep (one or more)	2
Fast food restaurant	1
Golfer	4
Lightning rod	2
Lake, pond, or river	1
Motorboat or rowboat	2
Deer (one or more)	3
Cows (one or more)	1

CAR LOTTO

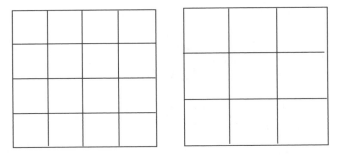

Players: 2–5
Equipment: A score card for each player,
prepared as described below
A pencil for each player
Preparation: Make each score card into a lotto
card that looks like this:

Fill in each box with the name of a different
person or thing in the desired category. Each
card should be somewhat different. You can
use the individual items on more than one
card, but put them in a different order.

This game takes a bit of preparation, but it's worth it. The idea is that you set up your own lotto cards before the trip starts, with special items on them that you'll encounter as you drive along.

For instance, you could fill in the boxes with some of the items in the Eagle Eye list on page 74 that you'll see as you drive. Or you could fill the boxes with the names of the singers you're likely to hear on the car radio.

It might look like this:

Bjork	Britney Spears	Michael Jackson
Madonna	David Bowie	Natalie Cole
Frank Sinatra	Ricky Martin	The Beatles

Then, when you're ready to start, turn on the radio. As each singer comes on, the players with that performer on their cards cross the name out. The first player to cross out a name in every box in a row—horizontally, vertically, or diagonally—wins.

This game will work with other categories, too. You can play it with musical groups, individual musicians, commercials, subjects on the news, makes of cars, popular songs, and famous people.

War	Stocks	Accidents
Animals	Films	Weather
Schools	Television	Health

Here is another sample card:

Bank	Food	Beverage
Restaurant	clothing	Beauty product
Automobile	Entertainment	Health product

FLASH CATEGORIES

Players: 2–6
Equipment: A dozen or more small cards or
sturdy paper cut down to business card size
Preparation: On each card write the name of a
classification such as Flowers, Gems,
Months, States, Countries, Articles of
Clothing, Television Programs, Colors,
Operas, Playwrights, Composers, Artists, etc.

Shuffle the cards and place the pack face-down.

The player who goes first calls out a letter of the alphabet, turns up the top card, and reads it aloud.

Then each player tries to name something in the category that starts with the letter that was called. The first one to think of an object gets the card. It might go like this:

KRISTIN: G. *(Turning up the top card)* Monster.

NEAL: Godzilla. *(Kristin gives him the card and the pack. It is now Neal's turn. He takes a card from the top of the pack and reads.)* Cartoon character.

ERIC: Gilligan. *(He takes the card from Neal, and the pack; he reads the top card from the pack)* Hero. *(No one can think of a hero beginning with G, so the card goes back to the bottom of the pack and Eric takes another card from the top. But this time he changes the letter.)* S. *(Reads top card)* Actor.

NEAL: George C. Scott.

And so on. Play the game until all the cards are won (if possible). The player with the greatest number of cards wins.

Keep the cards in your car's glove compartment. You can use them over and over to play "Flash Categories."

81

NIGHT RIDER

Players: 2 or more
Equipment: None
Preparation: None

There are plenty of car games to play by day when there's a great deal to look at, but when it's night and you're on a dull road—and feeling a little dull yourself—what do you play? "Night Rider," of course! It's a different kind of game, because nobody wins. Nobody can. All you have to do is make a sound, a different sound, whenever a particular situation comes up.

When a car passes you, for example, everyone says BZZZ, BZZZ, BZZZ. When you pass another car, everyone says, EEEE, EEEE, EEEE.

Here are a few of the most common "events" and the sounds that go with them:

CAR PASSES: BZZZ BZZZ
YOU PASS CAR: EEEE EEEE EEEE
YOU GO OVER A BRIDGE: OOOO OOOO OOOO
YOU GO UNDER A BRIDGE OR UNDERPASS: AYE AYE AYE
YOU PASS SIGN: AHHH AHHH AHHH
YOU PASS TRUCK: WHEE WHEE WHEE
TRUCK PASSES YOU: WOOF WOOF WOOF

As you get used to playing the game, you'll want to make up other sounds to go with other happenings. Different types of signs could call for different responses. Trailers, cars pulling boats, and motorcycles could each get sounds of their own. and the players take turns choosing what sound goes with what.

Silly? You bet. Especially when three or four of these events take place at the same time. You're going over a bridge, say, and there's a sign saying Exit 16, and a truck passes you, and it comes out:

OOOO OOOO OOOO AHHH AHHH AHHH WOOF WOOF WOOF

The more people who play the game the better, and the noisier.

Of course, after you play this game a few times, you may find yourself barking every time a truck passes you in heavy traffic—and that could be a bit difficult to explain—but that's one of the risks you take....

3 Travel Songs

The songs in this section are the best songs—
the best we know of, anyway—for singing in
the car.

You sing these when you're coming to the end of the trip—continually—until you get there.

WE'RE HERE

....

(sung to the tune of "Auld Lang Syne")

We're here because we're here,
Because we're here, because we're here.
We're here because we're here,
Because we're here, because we're here.

There's the famous walking song:

99 MILES

Oh, I'm 99 miles from home,
I'm 99 miles from home,
I walk a while and rest a while,
I'm 99 miles from home....

And then, "I'm 98 miles from home...." and so on until you get there, or until you can't stand it anymore.

And another song that repeats and repeats:

AROUND THE CORNER
....

Around the corner and under a tree—
A sergeant major once said to me,
"Who would marry you?
I would like to know,
For every time I look at your face
It makes me want to go—
Around the corner....

And so on and so on and on and on and on.

There are also the many verse songs for hiking, such as:

THE ANTS GO MARCHING

(to the tune of "When Johnny Comes Marching Home")
The ants go marching one by one,
    hurrah, hurrah,
The ants go marching one by one,
    hurrah, hurrah,
The ants go marching one by one,
The little one stops to suck his thumb
And they all go marching, out in the big
    parade.

Then the ants go marching:

2×2: The little one stops to tie his shoe
3×3: The little one stops to climb a tree
4×4: The little one stops to sleep some more
5×5: The little one stops to joke and jive
6×6: The little one stops to do some tricks
7×7: The little one stops to point to heaven
8×8: The little one stops to shut the gate
9×9: The little one stops to read a sign
10×10: The little one stops to say
THE END

And stop singing!

And then there are songs for which you contribute your own verse while everyone else sings the chorus, such as "You Can't Get to Heaven." If the people on the bus or in the car would like to, they can come up with their own verses, but here are a bunch to keep you going for miles.

YOU CAN'T GET TO HEAVEN

Oh, you can't get to heaven
(the group sings: Oh, you can't get to heaven)
On roller skates
(On roller skates)
Cause you'll roll right by
(cause you'll roll right by)
Those pearly gates!
(Those pearly gates!)

Chorus: Oh, you can't get to heaven
On roller skates
Cause you'll roll right by
Those pearly gates—
Oh, I ain't a-gonna grieve—
My lord no more!

Oh, I ain't gonna grieve
My lord no more!
I ain't gonna grieve
My lord no more!
Oh, I ain't a-gonna grieve—
My lord no more!

Oh, you can't get to heaven
In a rocking chair
Cause the rocking chair,
Won't get you there.

Oh, you can't get to heaven
In a trolley car
Cause the gosh darn thing
Won't go that far.

Oh, you can't get to heaven
On a rocket ship
Cause the rocket ship
Won't make the trip.

Oh, you can't get to heaven
In a limousine
Cause the Lord don't sell
No gasoline.

Oh, you can't get to heaven
With fear and doubt
Cause the Lord wants you
To cast them out.

Oh, you can't get to heaven
On a pizza pie
Cause the pizza pie
Won't fly that high.

WHOOOAAAAAAAAA

Oh, you can't get to heaven
On brand-new wheels
Cause the Lord won't make
No discount deals.

Oh, you can't get to heaven
On a pair of skis
Cause you'll schuss right through
St. Peter's knees.

Oh, you can't get to heaven
With chocolate chips
Cause the Lord don't like
Them on your hips.

Oh, you can't get to heaven
With powder and paint
Cause the Lord don't like
You as you ain't.

Oh, you can't get to heaven
With Superman
Cause the Lord he is
A Batman fan.

If you get to heaven
Before I do
Just bore a hole
And pull me through.

If I get to heaven
Before you do
I'll plug that hole
With shavings and glue.

That's all there is,
There ain't no more,
St. Peter said,
And closed the door.

A similar song is "Aiken Drum," in which each singer contributes a different part of Aiken Drum and what it is made of, and then everyone sings the chorus together.

AIKEN DRUM

Oh, his hair was made of cream cheese,
Of cream cheese,
Of cream cheese,
And his hair was made of cream cheese,
And his name was Aiken Drum.
Chorus: And he played upon a ladle,
A ladle, a ladle,
And he played upon a ladle
And his name was Aiken Drum.

And his eyes were made of golf balls,
Of golf balls,
Of golf balls,
And his eyes were made of golf balls,
And his name was Aiken Drum.

(And so on, right through Aiken Drum's whole body.)

101

And then there are songs where you keep adding on, like "Old MacDonald."

OLD MACDONALD

Old MacDonald had a farm,
E-I-E-I-O.
And on that farm he had a duck,
E-I-E-I-O.

And everyone sings the chorus:
Chorus: With a quack-quack here
And a quack-quack there,
Here a quack, there a quack,
Everywhere a quack-quack—
Old MacDonald had a farm, E-I-E-I-O.

(The singers each take turns adding in an animal on the farm.)

THIS SONG
QUACKS
ME UP!!.

Old MacDonald had a farm,
E-I-E-I-O.
And on that farm he had a cow,
E-I-E-I-O.
Chorus: With a moo-moo here
And a moo-moo there,
Here a moo, there a moo,
Everywhere a moo-moo—

But you add on all the previous animals, in backwards order, when you sing the chorus:

With a quack-quack here
And a quack-quack there,
Here a quack, there a quack,
Everywhere a quack-quack,
Old MacDonald had a farm,
E-I-E-I-O.

pig:	oink oink
horse:	neigh neigh
chicken:	cluck cluck
sheep:	baa baa
dog:	woof woof
snake:	hiss hiss
wolf:	howl howl
owl:	hoot hoot
mule:	hee haw
dove:	coo coo
rooster:	cock-a-doodle-doo
crow:	caw caw
bird:	tweet tweet

Then there are the elimination songs like "Bingo," in which you leave out another letter every time you sing it and just clap instead. The fun is in the sounds you *don't* sing together:

BINGO

There was a farmer had a dog
And Bingo was his name, oh!
B-I-NGO, B-I-NGO, B-I-NGO
And Bingo was his name, oh!

There was a farmer had a dog
And Bingo was his name, oh!
(*Clap*) I-NGO, (*Clap*) I-NGO,
(*Clap*) I-NGO,
And Bingo was his name, oh!

And so on, until you are singing:

There was a farmer had a dog
And Bingo was his name, oh!
*(Clap, clap, clap clap clap,
Clap, clap, clap clap clap,
Clap, clap, clap clap clap),*
And Bingo was his name, oh!

Don't forget the great rounds that sound so marvelous as you sing them together. It's important, though, that everyone know them *very well* so each person can hold the melody and isn't sidetracked by other—maybe stronger—singers. For that reason, the most well-known songs are the winners. Try them.

THREE BLIND MICE

Three blind mice,
Three blind mice,
See how they run,
See how they run.
They all run after the farmer's wife,
She cuts off their tails with a carving knife,
Did you ever see such a sight in your life—-
As three blind mice.

MERRILY WE ROLL ALONG

Merrily we roll along
Roll along, roll along,
Merrily we roll along
O'er the deep blue sea.

ROW, ROW, ROW YOUR BOAT

Row, row, row your boat
Gently down the stream,
Merrily, merrily, merrily, merrily,
Life is but a dream.

FRERE JACQUES

Frère Jacques, Frère Jacques,
Dormez-vous?
Dormez-vous?
Sonnez les matines, sonnez les matines,
Ding, dong, ding,
Ding, dong, ding.

KOOKABURRA

The Kookaburra is a bird, an Australian king-fisher with a loud, crazy-sounding call. This classic song makes a great round.

Kookaburra sits in the old gum tree,
Merry merry king of the bush is he.
Laugh, Kookaburra, laugh, Kookaburra,
Gay your life must be.

OH, HOW LOVELY IS THE EVENING

When you sing this well-known song as a round, it has a haunting sound, like bells echoing in the twilight.

Oh, how lovely is the evening,
Is the evening,
When the bells are sweetly ringing,
Sweetly ringing,
Ding, dong
Ding, dong —

And repeat.

And finally, the famous end-of-vacation song:

TEN MORE DAYS OF VACATION

Ten more days of vacation,
Then we go back to the station,
Back to civilization—
We don't want to go home!

We don't want to go home!
We don't want to go home!
We want to stay right here.

Then you sing, "Nine more days of vacation,"
and then "Eight more days of vacation," until
you come to the end:

No more days of vacation,
Now we go back to the station,
Back to civilization—
Now we have to go home.

And there are hundreds of other songs that help make long trips shorter. Singing is probably the best entertainment of all for motor trips, because everyone can take part all the time, and it's wonderful for many other situations as well. Few things make you feel better. Try your own favorites.

4 Wonderful Word Games

Some of the games in this section are classic games you've been playing for years, but it just wouldn't be right to leave them out.

GHOST AND DOUBLE GHOST

Players: 2–4
Equipment: None
Preparation: None

"Ghost" is a game of word building. The first player says a letter—any letter—that begins a word, and the next player adds a letter to it. The object of the game is to force one of the other players to complete a word by the addition of a letter, and to avoid forming a complete word yourself. Three-letter words don't count.

The player who ends the word gets the "G" of the word *ghost*. The second miss makes for an "H" and the third an "O." Whoever becomes a G-H-O-S-T first loses.

You must have a word in mind when you add a letter to the word-in-process. If the next player can't think of a word that can be formed from the letters already given, you

may be challenged. Then, if you can produce a word, it counts as a miss for the challenger. If you are bluffing, with no real word in mind, you lose and become a step closer to becoming a ghost.

Well, that's plain "Ghost." "Double Ghost" is tougher.

DOUBLE GHOST

The first player starts by giving two letters. The next player can add one letter either at the beginning or at the end. For example:

JOE: RT.

FLO: ORT.

JOE: ORT-H.

FLO *(doesn't want to make it NORTH, but NORTHERLY is a word)*: ORTH-E.

JOE: ORTHE-R.

FLO *(suddenly realizing that NORTHERLY would end on her, but that NORTHERN will end on Joe)*: ORTHER-N.

JOE *(hoping that Flo will not think of the word NORTHERNMOST, and will challenge him)*: ORTHERN-M.

And the game continues until NORTHERNMOST is reached and Joe becomes a G of a ghost.

SUPER GHOST

••

Only for people with great vocabularies. Try playing "Double Ghost" starting with two letters and adding two letters each time!

WORD STRINGS

Players: 2 or more
Equipment: None
Preparation: None

You play this game in the same way you play "Ghost," but you don't have to stop once you complete a word—if you can come up with a letter that builds the word further. The object of the game is to keep adding letters until the word can no longer be increased. Example:

ANNE: H.
BILL: A.
CATHY: P.
DANA: P.
ANNE: E.
BILL: N. *(Bill would now be a G in an ordinary game of "Ghost," but in this game,*

Cathy is the one who would get the G if she couldn't continue the word. But she can.)

CATHY: S.

DANA *(will he do it?)*: T. *(He did it.)*

ANNE: A

BILL: N.

CATHY: C.

DANA: E.

ANNE *(can't think of any way to continue):* Okay, I'm a G.

I LOVE MY LOVE WITH AN A

Players: 2 or more
Equipment: None
Preparation: None

Remember "A My Name Is Alice"? Well, this is a more complex version of it.

The first player starts:

"I love my love with an A because he is *adventurous.* I loathe my love with an A because he is *annoying.* His name is *Albert.* He lives in *Australia,* and he *adores ants* that he feeds *applesauce.*"

So, you see it's a little more complicated than "A My Name Is," but it's the same idea.

Instead of filling in four blanks (A my name is *Alice* and my husband's name is *Albert.* We live in *Australia* and we sell *apples*), you fill in six slightly more demanding ones:

❑ 2 adjectives *(adventurous* and *annoying)*, which can be fun

❑ the usual name of the person and place *(Albert* and *Australia)*. a silly hobby or occupation in two words *(adoring ants)*

❑ a silly activity (feeding them *applesauce)*

The second player continues with B:

"I love my love with a B because he is *bold*.
I loathe my love with a B because he is *boring*.
His name is *Bart*. He lives in *Burbank* and he
beats bears when he takes them *bowling*.

DANCE DARINGLY IN DENMARK

Players: 2 or more
Equipment: None
Preparation: None

"A My Name is Alice" has endless variations. Here's another complex version that has some style.

The first player starts with A, saying, "I'm taking a trip to _____ (Afghanistan, for example). What will I do there?"

Player #2 must answer with a verb and another word beginning with the same letter as the name of the place.

"Act arrogant in Afghanistan" would be a possible answer.

Then Player #2 poses the B question: "I'm taking a trip to Barcelona," he might say. "What will I do there?"

Player #3 might answer, "Bake biscuits in Barcelona," and then throw a C to Player #4, who may recommend catching chimpanzees in Canberra, and so on.

The game continues through the alphabet. If players can't come up with a question or an answer within a reasonable time, they get one count against them. Three counts and they're out of the game. Winner is the last one left.

SNIP!

Players: 2 or more
Equipment: None
Preparation: None

Traditionally, "Snip!" is played with a knotted handkerchief. The one who is "It" starts the game by throwing the hanky to one of the other players. But if you're not in a place where you can throw hankies around, you can just point—or if there are only two of you, take turns.

In any case, as you throw the handkerchief, or just before you point, call out a word of three letters. Then, as soon as the hanky is caught by one of the players, or immediately after you point, start counting to 12.

The player who got the handkerchief (or is pointed at) must respond with three words that begin with any of the letters in the word you called out. And the player must do it before you can finish counting. Because when you get to 12 and yell "Snip!" the player is out.

For example, let's say you call out the word "Man" and point a finger at David. He has to use letters M, A, and N. He could shout, "Make A Nightgown," or "Mean And Nutty," or just three unrelated words, such as "Money, Alligator, Necktie."

But whatever David replies, he has to get out the last word before you finish counting to 12. If David does it successfully, he becomes "It."

If you want to make the game more difficult, you can decide beforehand that every player must come up with related words, or even a full sentence. But more players will get snipped that way, which might make the game fairly short.

If only two are playing, let every snip count one point in favor of the snipper. Three snips wins.

129

GEOGRAPHY

Players: 2 or more
Equipment: None
Preparation: None

This is an ideal game to play on a motor trip, especially if you're the one holding the map—and it is the basis for dozens of other games!

In basic "Geography," the person who starts the game gives the name of a city or state or country or island or body of water or mountain. It is up to the next person to name another place, one whose name begins with the same letter that the first place ended with.

Here is a sample game:

CYD: Brisbane.
ROBERT: England.
BARBARA: Denmark.
CARLOS: Kentucky.
JEAN: York.

When a player can't think of a place that begins with the right letter, that player is out. The game continues until there is just one person left in it, the winner.

Words like "islands," "rivers," and "mountains" are not allowed. You wouldn't say "the Philippine Islands," for example, but "the Philippines." You wouldn't say "Nile River," but "the Nile," and words like "the" and "an" don't count. It's also "Everest," and not "Mount Everest."

No place name may be said more than once.

Since, after the game has been going for a while, some players take a very long time coming up with a name, it is a good idea to set a time limit. The shorter the time limit, the more interesting the game.

Hint: One of the problems with this game is that when you get started naming places beginning with A, it seems that most of them end with A, and the game can get bogged down.

TURN LEFT AT THE NEXT FOLD!

Here are some A's that don't end in A, to use when you need them.

Aberdeen
Abilene
Abingdon
Acapulco
Adelaide
Adrian
Afghanistan
Aiken
Alamo
Albany
Albion
Albuquerque
Alderney
Aldershot
Aleutians, the
Algiers
Alice Springs
Allentown
Alsace
Amalfi

Amarillo
Amazon
Ames
Amherst
Amsterdam
Anaheim
Anchorage
Anderson
Andes
Andover
Annapolis
Ann Arbor
Antibes
Antioch
Antwerp
Anzio
Appalachians,
  the
Arctic Circle
Arctic, the

Arezzo
Arkansas
Armentières
Armidale
Arnheim
Arno, the
Arroyo
  Grande
Ashland
Asheville
Assisi
Athens
Atlantic City
Atlantic, the
Auburn
Austin
Avignon
Avon, the
Ayers Rock
Azores, the

There also seems to be a shortage of Es, because so many place names end with them. Here are a few to remember:

Easter Island	Elmhurst	Estonia
Easthampton	Elmira	Ethiopia
East Lynn	Elmwood	Etna
Easton	El Paso	Eton
Ecuador	El Salvador	Euclid
Eden	Encino	Eureka
Edinburgh	Endicott	Europe
Edison	Enfield	Euston
Edmond	England	Evanston
Edmondton	Englewood	Evansville
Egypt	Enid	Everett
Elba	Enterprise	Everglades
Eldorado	Erie	Evergreen
Elgin	Erin	Evran
Elizabeth	Erskine	Excelsior
Elkton	Escondido	Exeter
Ellendale	Essen	Exmoor
Ellsworth	Essex	Eyre

There may be times when you need an X. Here are a few—and where they are located—in case you are challenged:

Xabregas (Portugal)
Xambioa (Brazil)
Xanten (Germany)
Xanthi (Greece)
Xenia (Illinois)
Xenia (Ohio)
Xeros (Cyprus)
Xertigny (France)

Xhoris (Belgium)
Xime (Guinea)
Xinavane (Mozambique)
Xinia (Greece)
Xochimilco (Greece)

X MARKS THE SPOT!

OTHER END GAMES

You can play "Geography" with any other subject your group is interested in. If you're into theatre or film, you can do it with plays or movies. For example:

Abby: Titanic.
Barry: Country Girl.
Carol: Lolita.
Dan: American Beauty.
Abby: You've Got Mail.

You can play it with songs if you're into music, with characters in books, with athletes' names, or with the names of movie stars. Make up your own rules to ease your way over the rough spots (like the A and E in "Geography").

PHRASE GEOGRAPHY

In addition to playing "Geography" with letters, you can play it in a slightly different way with phrases. Each word used needs to be part of a phrase, like TOP HAT or UPSIDE DOWN.

A sample game might go like this:

NAN: House.
DAN: House cat.
NAN: Cat call.
DAN: Call back.
NAN: Back rub.
DAN: Rub down.
NAN: Down hill.
DAN: Hillside.
NAN: Side kick.
DAN: Kick boxing.
NAN: Boxing ring.
DAN: Ring toss.
NAN: Toss up.

UPSIDE DOWN HILL!

THE MISSING LETTER

Players: 2 or more
Equipment: None
Preparation: None

The game seems simple, but it's deceptive.

All you have to do is ask the other player a question and then mention a single letter of the alphabet. Your opponent must answer your question with a sentence that does not use the letter at all.

Answers may be serious or silly. Then it is the next player's turn to ask a question leaving out a specific letter. Simple? Wait till you try to express yourself without the letter E or the letter S! Writing the answers instead of speaking them makes it easier, but not much!

Here are some sample questions and answers.

What did you do last summer? E.
Nothing much, it was dark.

What do you put in your pen? I.
We use pea soup.

What do you live in? H.
I live in a large zoo.

HINKY PINKY

Players: 2 or more
Equipment: None
Preparation: None

You can play "Hinky Pinky" anywhere and any time. A hinky pinky is a phrase made up of two-syllable rhyming words, such as "silly filly."

In order to play, all you have to do is define your Hinky Pinky, and the other player must guess what it is. For example, you might define "silly filly" as a "ditzy horse." Or you might say you had a hinky pinky that meant an unpleasant part of the face. The other player would have to guess that was a "horrid forehead."

Here are a few hinky pinkies. Can you figure them out? Answers on page 344.

1. Fowl that wins the lottery
2. Powerful sleepwear
3. Revolting couple
4. Hamlet's mother
5. A less healthy heart

6. A wicked insect
7. Small space vehicle
8. A fat ape
9. A hen who works in a chorus line
10. A scribble made by a piece of pasta

If you want to add to the game, you can try hink pinks, too. A hink pink is a shorter hinky pinky, made up of two one-syllable words, such as "fat cat." Here are some hink pinks:

1. An enormous boat
2. An ape who overeats compulsively
3. A hen who has a bad cold
4. What rodents have when they get together to talk
5. A vulgar thoroughbred
6. A sad buddy
7. What you have when your boat sinks in the middle of a huge lake
8. A vegetable that has it all together
9. A sneaky insect
10. A bird who is not very bright

It's as much fun to make up hinky pinkies as it is to guess them. Maybe more.

Answers on page 344.

5 Nutty Games

Many of the games in the previous chapters are funny, but the ones in this section have a special nuttiness to them. They're all different, all kind of silly, and all a lot of fun to play. In fact, part of the fun is seeing how silly they can get!

HEADLINES

Players: 5 or more
Equipment: A sheet of paper or small pad for
*   every player*
Preparation: None

Fewer than five can play this game, but the more players the more fun it is.

A leader reads a list of four or five letters of the alphabet. Each person is to write a message using these letters as the first letters of each word, in the order the letters are read.

For example, suppose the letters given are A, B, E, and W. One message might read, "A Bear Eats Woodchucks." Another might be "Annie Bathes Every Winter," or "Anxious Baboons Explore World."

After the players have finished making up their headlines, they take turns reading them out loud, and that's the best part.

Note: After using easy letters to begin with, you can slip in some harder ones—Q, J and Y, for example—and the messages will get even sillier and funnier.

THE WOOLLCOTT GAME

Players: 2 or more
Equipment: Pencil and paper
  A watch or clock (digital or with a sweep
  second hand)
Preparation: None

Alexander Woollcott, the famous American author and critic, has been credited with inventing this one-minute game for two.

Your opponent keeps score and does the timing while you concentrate for 60 seconds. During that minute, you must say all the words that you can that start with a given letter. That's all there is to it.

Sounds easy, doesn't it? Well, try it.

The timekeeper says, "Start when I give you the letter—R," and then starts the clock. As you call off words that begin with R, the timekeeper keeps track of them by marking them off in groups of 5, like this: ‖‖‖

Of course, the dictionary is packed with common—and uncommon—words beginning with every letter of the alphabet, but you'll be surprised how difficult it is to think of them as you sit there faced by that relentless second hand, not to mention the note-taking timekeeper.

When the minute is up, total up the number of words you called out and then change roles. Give each other letters of similar ease or difficulty (see below). If you get a Z, you're entitled to give a Y, but an S deserves a C.

Order of frequency as a starting letter:

S - C - P - A- B - T- M - D - R - H - E- F - L - G - I - W - N - O - U - V - K - J - Q - Y - Z - X.

BACKWARD ALPHABET

Players: 2 or more
Equipment: Watch with a second hand
Preparation: None

Each player in turn recites the alphabet backwards. The one who can do it fastest is the winner. The other players watch for omissions, and anyone skipping a letter is out.

I'M FEELING A LITTLE *BACKWARD* TODAY!

FROZEN YOGURT

Players: 2 or more
Equipment: None
Preparation: None

Think of a noun and keep it secret while the other players try to guess what it is. They ask questions about anything they want. You answer all their questions any way you like—truthfully or untruthfully—but in every answer you have to mention the secret noun. How can you mention it and keep it secret at the same time? Because instead of actually saying the noun, you say, "Frozen yogurt."

For example, if the secret noun were "ghost," the game might go like this:

MICHELE: How do you feel today?
YOU: Not as bad as a frozen yogurt.
SONJA: What is your favorite thing to do?
YOU: Tell frozen yogurt stories.
MIKE: Where are you going for the holidays?
YOU: Out west to visit a frozen yogurt town.
JOHN: What's your favorite movie?
YOU: Frozen Yogurt Busters.
MICHELE: What's your favorite song?
YOU: "I Don't Stand a Frozen Yogurt of a Chance with You."

Well, that one probably gave it away.

The first person to guess what the frozen yogurt stands for chooses the next subject.

Any player who guesses incorrectly drops out of the round. If nobody guesses, you get to choose another noun.

If frozen yogurt doesn't appeal to you, substitute something else, like a pepperoni pizza, an onion bagel, or a Belgian waffle.

YOUR MONKEY'S MUSTACHE

Players: 2
Equipment: None
Preparation: None

This game is similar to "Frozen Yogurt" because you keep saying a phrase over and over again in answer to questions, but it's a different type of game. the object here is to keep from laughing.

One person is "It." The others select a phrase that "It" must answer to every question. The group could pick "Your monkey's mustache," or "Six smelly sneakers," or "Uncle Andy's underwear," or anything you like.

Then each person in the group gets to ask a question, such as "What are you going to have for dinner tonight?" or "Who did you spend most of your time with last summer?" Of course, the questions are tailored to be as hilarious as possible when answered by the phrase picked out beforehand. And if "It" laughs, "It" is out. Winner is the biggest grouch.

BUZZ

Players: 2 or more
Equipment: None
Preparation: None

"Buzz" is a simple counting game, and the players take turns counting from 1 up to 100. But the catch is that instead of saying any number that has a 7 in it, or is a multiple of 7, you have to say BUZZ.

So that means that you have to say BUZZ instead of any of the following numbers: 7, 14, 17, 21, 27, 28, 35, 37, 42, 47, 49, 56, 57, 63, 67, 70, 71, 72, 73, 74, 75, 76, 77 (you need to say BUZZ-BUZZ for this one), 78, 79, 84, 87, 91, 97, 98.

Anyone who doesn't say BUZZ when any of these numbers comes up, or who says BUZZ when he or she shouldn't, is out of the game.

FIZZ BUZZ

A variation on "Buzz," "Fizz Buzz" is tougher, but a lot more fun. You still have to say BUZZ whenever a 7 or its multiple comes up, but now instead of 5 and its multiples, you have to say FIZZ.

So the following numbers are FIZZ: 5, 10, 15, 20, 25, 30, 35, 40, 45, 50, 51, 52, 53, 54, 55 (FIZZ-FIZZ), 56, 57, 58, 59, 60, 65, 70, 75, 80, 85, 90, 95, 100.

But be careful: 35, 56, 57, 70, and 75 are also BUZZ. So 35 becomes BUZZ-FIZZ; 56 and 57 become FIZZ-BUZZ; and 70 and 75 become BUZZ-FIZZ.

This game can be hilarious.

155

CHEESEBURGER

Players: 2 or more
Equipment: None
Preparation: None

This great variation on "Buzz" was introduced in a skit on *Saturday Night Live*.

The players count off in regular order, but instead of saying Buzz for number 7, you say "Cheeseburger" (pronounced CHIZ-bugga).

When you get to 70, though, you say:

Cheeseburger-one
Cheeseburger-two
Cheeseburger-three
Cheeseburger-four
Cheeseburger-five
Cheeseburger-cheeseburger
Cheeseburger-cheeseburger
Cheeseburger-eight
Cheeseburger-nine

So it's pretty tricky!

Anyone who hesitates, misses, or says, "Seven" or any multiple of it is out.

If you want to get even trickier, keep saying "Cheeseburger" for 7, but also say "Pepsi" for 5 and any mulitples, so it goes:

1-2-3-4-Pepsi-6-Cheeseburger-8-9-Pepsi-11-12-13-Cheeseburger-Pepsi, and so on.

CHEESEBURGER WITH FRIES

Ready for more? If you're still hanging in there after all that, you can add "Fries" for 3, so it would go 1-2-Fries-4-Pepsi-Fries-Cheeseburger-8-Fries-Pepsi-11-Fries-Fries-Cheeseburger....and so on. It's practically impossible to do it with any kind of speed. This should be a riotous end to the game, no matter how skillful the players!

WOULD YOU LIKE FRIES WITH THAT?

TONGUE TWISTERS

Players: 1 or more
Equipment: A watch with a second hand
    Paper and pencil (optional)
Preparation: None

When you learned to talk, did you think anything would be physically impossible to say? Well, nothing is really physically impossible to say. You can master any tongue twister if you really practice it, say it slowly enough, and only say it once. But say it a few times quickly and you find your tongue playing ridiculous tricks on you.

You can make these tongue twisters into a game. They're short enough to be easy to remember when people don't have the book in front of them. See how many times the players can say each one correctly in 60 seconds.

Bake bad brown bread.

Chew two chopsticks.

Crisp snacks.

Eight eager eaglets escaped.

Fifty foxy fliers flew fast.

Flags fly freely.

Four fresh flying fish.

Fix it fast, Fess.

Hurry, Harry!

Mashed monkey meat.

Such cool sushi!

Swim, Sven!

Thick sliced or thin sliced?

Thirty overturned tractor trailer trucks.

Where do dreaded dwarfs dwell?

THOUGHTS

Players: 2 or more
Equipment: None
Preparation: None

You decide on a subject—some object, person, or idea—and don't tell the others what it is. Then you ask the other players, one by one, what your thought is like. The players can answer anything they like. They could say your thought is like Robin Williams, for example, or like a pickle, or like a sick elephant.

Then you tell them what your thought is and ask each player to defend the answer that was given.

For instance, you would say, "My thought was Napoleon. How is Robin Williams like Napoleon?"

And the player has to come up with some "reasonable" answer, such as, "They're both famous men who came from humble beginnings."

Or, when you ask, "How is a pickle like Napoleon?" the player might say, "Both of them sometimes are sour."

Or for "How is a sick elephant like Napoleon?" one jokester might say that they both may have had a code in the head.

The answer can be ridiculous—the more ridiculous the better—but if it doesn't make any sense at all, or if the players can't come up with any answer, they have to pay a forfeit or drop out of the game.

When all the players have had a chance to explain their answers, it's someone else's turn to be "It," and new thoughts are needed down the line.

THE MINISTER'S CAT

Players: 2 or more
Equipment: None
Preparation: None

This game is a very old one, and it seems so simple that you might wonder at first why anyone would want to play it. Then, after a few rounds, you fall under its spell and realize why it has been popular for so many years.

Usually the game is played in a circle, with each person taking turns. If you're traveling, of course, you can set up any order you want, but that order has to be the same all the time.

The leader starts by saying, "The minister's cat is a _____ cat," filling in the blank with an adjective beginning with A. The leader could say, for example, "The minister's cat is an abominable cat."

Then the turn passes to the next person, who comes up with another adjective beginning with A for the cat: "The minister's cat is an aggravating cat," for instance.

And so it goes. Endless, you say? You think it will go on forever because there are so many adjectives beginning with A? Well, yes, you'd think so. But very rapidly, especially if you don't let anyone miss a beat, people start stumbling, missing, going blank, repeating what's been said, stuttering, getting tongues twisted up, and saying words beginning with the wrong letter. All of which means that they are OUT. If your group is small, though, and you want to play a longer game, you can allow them three misses before they have to drop out.

In any case, when someone misses, everyone shifts to the next letter. The next person in turn would start with something like, "The minister's cat is a beautiful cat," or a bratty cat or a boring cat, etc.

THE MINISTER'S CAT IS ALL BAD

In this variation on the game, the adjectives all have to be negative. The minister's cat can't be agreeable, amiable, beautiful, bonny, charming, cute, or anything else pleasant. It can only be angry, awful, brash or bossy, cross or criminal, or otherwise a rotten pet. This makes the game much tougher and more fun.

THE MINISTER'S CAT IS INTERNATIONAL

In this variation, you decide that the minister's cat is always going to have a nationality:

JILL: The minister's cat is an African cat.
JACK: The minister's cat is a Belgian cat.
NED: The minister's cat is a Canadian cat.

Otherwise, all the rules are the same. A flub and you're out, or you get a count against you. Five counts and you're out.

A IS FOR AARDVARK

Players: 2 or more
Equipment: None
Preparation: None

This very silly alphabet game is another one of those quick contests that depends on your coming up with the right word at the right time.

CAROL: A is for Aardvark.
STAN: B bought it.
BILL: C cooked it.
PETE: D dunked it.
CAROL: E elevated it.
STAN: F flossed it.
BILL: G grasped it.
PETE: H handled it.
CAROL: I imitated it.
STAN: J jostled it.
BILL: K kissed it.

PETE: L loved it.
CAROL: M missed it.
STAN: N needed it.
BILL: O opened it.
PETE: P pinched it.
CAROL: Q questioned it.
STAN: R—R—.

Stan is out. And so it goes. Don't try for X, Y, and Z. If you want to play the game again, just outlaw using the same words. Or you can play it using longer answers, such as:

CAROL: A is for Aardvark.
STAN: B bought it candy.
BILL: C called it a dummy.
PETE: D did its hair.
CAROL: E embarrassed it.

And so on. The answers that the players come up with provide the entertainment in this one. Last person remaining in the game wins.

CATEGORIES

Players: 2 or more
Equipment: None
Preparation: None

Decide in what order the players will take their turns. Usually, the turns move around in a circle, but it depends on how you're seated. Any order will do, but it has to be the same all the time.

The players set up a six-beat rhythm. It goes like this:

❏ Tap your thighs twice.
❏ Clap your hands in front of you twice.
❏ Snap your fingers at about shoulder level twice.

All the players do this at the same time, and no one stops or misses a beat.

Now, when you've got the rhythm going well, the first player begins by saying, "Category" on one set of finger snaps, and then giving the title of a category on the next set of snaps. Categories should be broad—such as trees or fruits or flowers, TV shows, desserts, or breeds of dogs.

All the players keep up the tap-tap-clap-clap-snap-snap rhythm as the second player names something in the category on the next snap, ending the name by the time the second snap is over. Then the next player must give another name on the following snaps and so on, until somebody misses. It might go like this:

JANE *(tap-tap, clap-clap):* Category *(as all snap, tap-tap, clap-clap),* countries *(as they all snap).*

PAUL *(tap-tap, clap-clap):* England *(as they snap).*

KIT *(tap-tap, clap-clap):* Australia *(as they snap).*

CHRIS *(tap-tap, clap-clap):* Canada *(as they snap).*

JANE *(tap-tap, clap-clap):* United States *(as they snap).*

PAUL *(tap-tap, clap-clap):* Er— *(as they snap).*

Paul is OUT.

Everyone gets the rhythm going again and the next player, Kit, names a new category. Play on until only one person is left—the winner.

There's one more rule. You can't repeat a name that has already been given. That's no problem, you say? Well, wait until you're all set to say a particular thing and the player before you says it. You have about three seconds to come up with another name that hasn't been said before. Those snaps come fast, and it's hilarious to see the glazed eyes of a super-Categories player who has just dried up, blankly snapping fingers and not knowing what in the world is going to come out of his mouth! Remember, if your tongue gets tangled up—or you garble your answer—that's an automatic out, too!

THE UNDERHAND SLAP

••

Players: 2 or more
Equipment: None
Preparation: None

This terrific little contest is wonderful for those times when you're waiting around, standing on line, and don't want to play another word game.

Face your opponent, placing your hands out in front of you at waist level, with fingers lightly outstretched. Keep your palms down.

Your opponent puts his or her hands right under yours, palms up. Your palms and those of your opponent should barely touch. Now you stare into each other's eyes.

The object of this game is for the underhand opponent to whip his or her hands out and hit the backs of yours before you can get your hands away. In order to accomplish this, your opponent has to be very sly and very

fast, because the moment you get the idea
that you're about to get slapped, you're going
to get your hands out of there! How do you
know when you're going to get slapped? Not
only from the movement of the palms under
yours, but also from the gleam in the eye of

your opponent, a glint that is always there before a hit—unless you're dealing with a world-class underhand slapper!

Once you get hit, change positions and you become the underhand slapper.

Score two points for striking both hands, one for striking one hand. But the fun isn't in the score or the win. It's in that moment-to-moment eye-to-eye combat.

THE HOUSE THAT JACK BUILT

Players: 2 or more
Equipment: None
Preparation: None

This giggly sort of game is very like the nursery rhyme "The House That Jack Built." The first player makes a statement and the second player adds on a phrase. The players continue taking turns, and each one must repeat accurately all that has been said as well as adding a new phrase. None of the statements needs to be true, and the funnier the better.

For example:

I have a car.

I have a chauffeur who loves the car.

I have a maid who loves the chauffeur who loves the car.

I have a dish that was cracked by the maid who loves the chauffeur who loves the car.

I have a boy who smashed the dish that was cracked by the maid—and so on.

Any player who misses is out.

6 Pencil and Paper Games

From the familiar games you learned to play as a tot to the trickiest tactics, graphics, and word building, these pencil gymnastics will keep you busy for as long as you want. They're great for playing on the plane, easy to stop and start up again, and all you need, besides a paper and pencil, is a playmate in the next seat.

DOTS

Players: 2
Equipment: Pencil and paper
Preparation: None

Take a sheet of paper and make as many rows of dots as you want—10 or more dots in each direction. Then each player takes a turn and draws a line connecting one dot with the next in any direction—except diagonally—and in any part of the diagram.

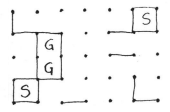

Try to connect the dots so that they make little squares. When you draw a line that finishes a square, you initial the closed square and then drawn an extra line. The player with the most initialed squares wins.

ETERNAL TRIANGLES

Players: 2
Equipment: Pencil and paper
Preparation: None

This game is similar to "Dots." Cover a sheet of paper with dots starting with one in the first row, two in the second, three in the third, and so on, as far as you care to go, as in the diagram below.

Each player in turn draws a line connecting two of the dots either horizontally or diagonally, and the object is to form an enclosed triangle. When you add the line that forms the enclosed triangle, initial it and go again. The game is over when one of you fails to form a triangle.

The player with the most triangles wins.

You can make this game more difficult if you score extra points for larger triangles—made up of small triangles with your initials only. Score them up at the end of the game.

SNAKES

Players: 2
Equipment: Pencil and paper
Preparation: None

Here is another relative of "Dots."

Set up a bunch of dots on your paper, the same way you did for the previous games. Now, starting anywhere you like, take turns drawing in lines from dot to dot, but don't make boxes. Instead make a long, stiff snake.

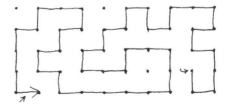

No diagonal lines are allowed. No skipping spaces.

The winner is the last one to be able to draw a line without connecting the snake to itself.

DOODLEBUG

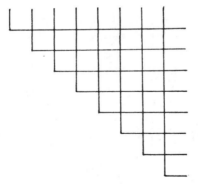

Players: 2
Equipment: Pencil and paper for each player
Preparation: None

Each player draws the following diagram:

Choose to see who goes first. The first player—Eve—writes a number between 1 and 8, not in one of the boxes, but elsewhere on her paper. She shields her pencil and paper with her other hand, hiding what she is writing from the other player, Adam.

If Adam can guess the number Eve wrote, he gets to write it in the appropriate line of his diagram, and it is his turn to write a hidden number.

If Adam guesses wrong, Eve gets to place the number on the appropriate line of her diagram, and she gets another turn.

The object of the game is to be the player who fills all the boxes of the diagram first. The diagram will then contain eight 8s, seven 7s, six 6s, etc.

Note: Cross off the hidden doodle numbers after each turn so that no arguments can arise about which number was just written.

Hint: When you doodle a number, either hold your pencil as still as possible so as not to give a clue to the number, or move it wildly to confuse your opponent.

BATTLESHIPS

. . . .

Players: 2

Equipment: Pencil and paper for each player
  (Use graph paper if available. It saves time
  and effort, and it's neater.)

Preparation: Each player makes up a 10-
  square chart (see next page)

The object of this popular game is to sink the
enemy's ships before the enemy can sink
yours.

Each player has:

❑ a battleship—made up of 5 squares
❑ a cruiser—made up of 4 squares
❑ a destroyer—made up of 3 squares
❑ a nuclear sub—made up of 2 squares

The first thing each player does is to hide
his/her ships in their charts. See the next page.

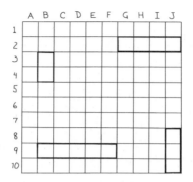

Ships can be placed horizontally or vertically, but not diagonally.

War is declared.

The first player—Jean—calls out a square by letter and number, say F5.

The other player—Mitch—must tell her whether or not it is a hit. Look at the sample game shown here. You'll see that it was a miss. Jean puts an O in that box, to show that it was called and it was a miss, so she won't call it again.

Now it's Mitch's turn. He calls B3, which just happens to be Jean's nuclear sub. Jean admits it is a hit, but she doesn't tell Mitch what *kind* of ship he hit. Mitch puts a big X in that square in his chart. Jean shades hers.

It's Jean's turn. She calls another square, D6—a hit, Mitch tells her. It is his destroyer, but he doesn't tell her that. Jean puts an X in D6. Mitch shades D6 in his chart.

Mitch's turn. He calls B4. Why? Mitch knows that at least one other square is connected to the first hit, since no ship fits in less than two squares. It is a hit. But this time, Jean must not only admit to the hit, she must admit that the ship is sunk.

Now Mike knows that he has sunk Jean's submarine, so he darkens in both submarine squares. He knows from that that he doesn't have to try to make any more hits right around that area. The next time Mitch's turn comes up, he'll be wise to call a square on the other side of the chart, or further down.

The charts now look like this:

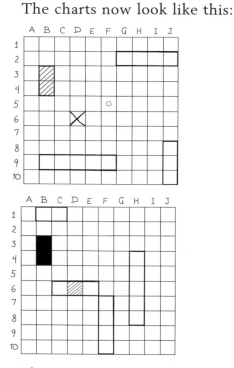

The game goes on in the same way until one player has sunk all the other player's ships.

About the charts: This game is often played with each player keeping up two charts, one to represent his or her own ships and the squares the enemy has called, and the other to show the calls the player has made and the hits scored. The two-chart method may be helpful when an adult is playing with a small child, who may mistakes in recording his or her own hits. Then the adult can help clear up any confusion. Otherwise, one chart seems to do the job very well.

HANGMAN

Players: 2
Equipment: Pencil and paper
Preparation: None

You need to know how to play "Hangman" in order to play "Hangman Grows Up." Just in case you don't know, here is a speedy explanation. (Also see the diagram.)

Draw a gallows (an upside-down L), think of a word (don't say it aloud), and dash off a string of dashes, one for each letter in the word. Then print the alphabet at the bottom of the page.

What your opponent must guess, one letter at a time, is the word you've chosen. If a guess of a letter is correct, write it at the appropriate place in the word, and strike it off in the alphabet below.

If the letter appears in your word more than once, put it in wherever it belongs.

If your opponent guesses wrong, strike the letter out of the alphabet and draw in a head at the end of the gallows rope.

For each wrong letter guessed, draw in another body part; two more wrong guesses would give two eyes. Another two would supply ears. A sixth would give a mouth, the seventh a torso, and the next four would add arms and legs.

D R A C U L A

A̶B̶C̶D̶E̶F G H I̶ J K L M̶ N O̶ P Q R̶S̶ T U̶ V W X Y Z

If you want to make the game longer, go on to hands and shoes.

Note: Long, complicated words are easier, not harder, than short words. Short words containing the less frequently used letters are the most difficult to guess, words such as *why*, *fox*, *bay*, *ski*, *tax*, and *yore*. Even if your opponent guessed o-r-e quickly, think of all the letters that would probably come up before getting to Y!

HANGMAN GROWS UP

Once you have become expert at "Hangman," you'll be ready for "Hangman Grows Up." Instead of just words, use other categories in the dashes. You might do it with proverbs, famous sayings, books, movies, or plays. How about famous people in history? Athletes? Song titles? The possibilities are endless. But because you get more clues than in regular "Hangman," two parts are hanged every time you miss.

DOUBLE HANGING

If an adult and child are playing together, they might want to try this variation on the game to make it more of a contest.

When it is the younger player's turn, he or she chooses two words and strings them out under the gallows. Then as the adult guesses, the younger one puts in the letters wherever they belong in both words. But when a letter appears in only one of the words, a part is hanged for the miss on the other word. If the letter appears in neither word, two parts are hanged.

TIC-TAC-TOE SQUARED

Players: 2
Equipment: Pencil and paper
Preparation: None

You probably know how to play "Tic-Tac-Toe" ("Noughts and Crosses"). It's played in a large square divided into nine small squares.

Each of two players in turn places his or her mark—an X or an O—in a small square.

The first player to get three marks in a horizontal, vertical or diagonal line wins.

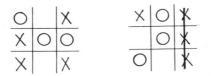

But "Tic-Tac-Toe Squared" will be a bit more of a challenge. Make the same tic-tac-toe box that you always make, but then close the edges:

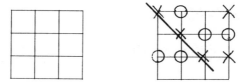

Play the Xs and Os on the intersections instead of in the boxes. You need three in a row to win.

TIC-TAC-TOE-TOE

If you get tired of "Tic-Tac-Toe Squared," try this variation. Draw five lines across and five lines down for a 4-box square playing area (16 boxes in all).

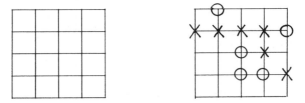

Play the Xs and Os on the intersection again, but this time you need four in a row to win.

GO-BANG

Players: 2–4
Equipment: Graph paper and
 Pencils
Preparation: None

There are lots of names for this game. People play it all over the world and call it something different. Even within the same country it is often called by several names.

You can play it on paper or on a pegboard with pegs or on a checkerboard—on any surface that is marked off in boxes. If you play it on paper, it is easier to use graph paper.

The object of the game is to take turns writing in Xs and Os, as in "Tic-Tac-Toe Squared," until you get five Xs or five Os in a row. If you are a skillful player, this game can go on and on!

Hint: Beware of a row of Xs and Os. When you see it, quickly stop it with your mark, because once your opponent gets four in a row—with nothing limiting it on either end—the game is over.

Three people or four can play this game, but it is best as a contest for two players. If you play with as many as four, use triangles and squares as well as Xs and Os.

CAT-ASTROPHE

Players: 2 or more
Equipment: Pencil and paper for each player
Preparation: None

For a long-playing pencil-and-paper game, choose a simple 3-letter word like "cat."

Set a time limit of from 15 to 30 minutes and, at a signal, start listing as many words as possible containing the word you've decided upon. The word may occur in any part of the longer word, but it must be intact.

For instance, if "cat" were your word, you could use *catastrophe*, *abdicate*, *prevaricate*, *scatter*, etc., but not *castle* or *intact*.

If you choose the word "pen," your list might contain *penny*, *repent*, *open*,etc.

The player with the longest list is the winner.

GIBBERISH

Players: 2
Equipment: Pencil and paper for each player
Preparation: None

Each player writes out a well-known proverb, running the letters all together, like this:

Astitchintimesavesnine.

Now break it up at odd intervals, like this:

Ast it chint imesa vesni ne.

Exchange papers and see who can be first to write out the proverb correctly. If you want to make the game last longer, each can write a number of proverbs, five apiece, or even ten— for the others to solve. You might find yourself looking at what seems to be a brand new conglomeration but turns out to be the same proverb you have given your opponent!

Here are some proverbs you can use for this game:

A bird in the hand is worth two in the bush.

A friend in need is a friend indeed.

Don't count your chickens until they're hatched.

Heaven helps those who help themselves.

205

One man's meat is another man's poison.
Necessity is the mother of invention.
A penny saved is a penny earned.
Absence makes the heart grow fonder.
Don't cry over spilt milk.
A watched pot never boils.
Birds of a feather flock together.
Actions speak louder than words.
Make hay while the sun shines.
The pen is mightier than the sword.

EVERY OTHER

Players: 2
Equipment: Pencil and paper for each player
Preparation: None

Crossword puzzle fans like playing this game. Armed with pencil and paper, each player makes out a list of ten words (or any number you agree on), but omits every other letter. To put it another way, write down every other letter, starting with the second letter of each word you've chosen. Next to each word, write a synonym or brief definition—preferably humorous or tricky. Then switch papers. Winner is the one with the most correct answers.

A sample list might contain:

- I - F - R - N - E meaning REMAINDER (*difference*)
- I - T - O - A - Y meaning WORDY BOOK (*dictionary*)

- A - H - O - A - L meaning OF THE LATEST STYLE *(fashionable)*

Set a time limit for each phase of the game, and after you've played it a few times, try playing without any definitions.

LONGEST WORD

Players: *2 or more*
Equipment: *Pencil and paper for each player*
Preparation: *None*

You start this game with a one-letter word (A or I) and add letters, one at a time. Each time you add a new letter it must form another word, and at no time can you change the order of the previous letters. But you may add the new letter at the beginning or the end, or insert it anywhere inside the word. The object is to see who can form the longest word.

When you arrive at the final word, tell it to your opponents, but don't let them see your worksheet. They must then play the game in reverse and take the letters away one by one until they arrive back at the original one-letter word.

Here is a sample game:
A
AY
SAY
STAY
STRAY
ASTRAY
ASHTRAY
ASHTRAYS

WORD STEPS

Players: 1 or more
Equipment: Pencil and paper for each player
Preparation: None

How many steps from "lamb" to "wolf"? We
made it in eight.

The idea is to progress from one word to another by changing one letter at a time. With each one-letter change, you must form a new word. For instance, this is one way to get from "lamb" to "wolf."

LAMB
LAME
SAME
SALE
SOLE
SOLD
GOLD
GOLF
WOLF

Maybe you can do it in fewer steps.

Start by selecting a pair of four-letter words at random—or you can choose a pair with amusing or contrasting association. All players write down the same pair of words and set a time limit of five or ten minutes. Now see who can get from one word to the other in the fewest steps. In case of a tie, the one who finishes first is the winner.

SPROUTS

Players: 2
Equipment: Pencil and paper
Preparation: None

This game is a bit like "Dots" (page 181) because you connect the dots, and because the object of the game is to leave your opponent unable to make a move.

But instead of a page full of dots, you start with just three or four anywhere on the page. And, in addition to straight lines, you can draw

arcs

curves

loops or

squiggles

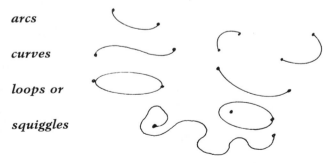

You can join two dots together, or make a loop joining one dot to itself.

Every time you draw a line, arc, curve, loop, or squiggle, you have to add a new dot (shown here as a larger white circle so you can see it more easily) somewhere on the line—*not* necessarily in the middle.

What's the catch? You may not cross a line

dotted line is illegal

and no blop may have more than three sprouts coming out of it. As soon as you attach your third sprout to the blop, put a slash through it (it makes it easier to see) so that you know that blop is out of play.

When you get expert, you may decide to leave the slashes out.

The winner is the one who makes the last possible move.

Part of the fun of "Sprouts" is that while you're sprouting and blopping, you're creating a very weird picture. Try it!

Here is a game you might play:

lst move

2nd move

3rd move

4th move

5th move

6th move

Even though two blops are still alive, you cannot play them without crossing a line or connecting to a dead blop. The game is over.

7th move

I'M REALLY MAD!!

I'VE CROSSED THE LINE!..

WORD BRIDGES

Players: 2
Equipment: Pencil and paper for each player
Preparation: None

Be an architect of words and see who can build the longest word bridge with pencil and paper.

Each player draws six horizontal lines across the paper and then one gets first choice in selecting a word of six letters. Write the word vertically down the page, one letter at the beginning of each line. Then write the word up from the bottom, one letter at the end of each line.

```
F . . . . . . . . . . . . R
E . . . . . . . . . . . . E
N . . . . . . . . . . . . D
D . . . . . . . . . . . . N
E . . . . . . . . . . . . E
R . . . . . . . . . . . . F
```

Each game lasts three minutes. At the word "Go" you each start to fill in the six bridges with words starting and ending with the letters that are already there. the longer the word, the better. When the game is over, you score as follows:

The player with the longest word for each bridge gets 5 points. Then add up the total number of letters used for all six words. The player with the highest total score subtracts the next highest score and adds the difference to his or her total score.

The first player to win 50 points, or 100 points if you want to play a longer game, is the winner.

7 At the Table

How many times, especially when you're traveling and have to eat out a lot, have you been stuck at the table when you don't want to be? It happens while you wait for your order to be taken, while you wait for your food to be served, while you wait for dessert, while you wait for the bill. You can play these games while you're doing all that waiting, if the people you're sitting with don't object.

MAKING A PAPER CUP YOU CAN DRINK FROM

....

Players: 1
Equipment: A sheet of paper (square)
Preparation: See page 222.

No, this isn't a game, but it's such a valuable thing to know how to do that it belongs in any book about traveling.

Have you ever been stuck without a cup or glass? It happens quite a lot. Sometimes the hotel or motel doesn't leave enough glasses. Sometimes you fill them with something else. Or maybe you want to scoop up some water from a fountain or a stream, or get a drink from someone else's bottled water. This is how to make your own paper cup that will hold water, and all you need is one sheet of paper.

The ideal sheet of paper for making the paper cup is 8½" (216mm) square. Where do you get a sheet that weird size? You can of course measure it out and cut it, if you have a ruler and scissors. But if not and you have two sheets of 8½ × 11 notebook paper (280mm × 216mm), use one of the sheets to measure off 8½ inches against the other like this:

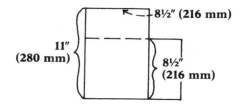

1. Fold the sheet diagonally.

2. Take the top end (a) and fold it (dotted line) so that it meets the center of the opposite side (d).

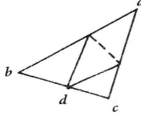

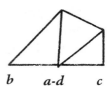

3. Make a sharp crease. Turn over the folded sheet. It looks a little like a kite.

4. Fold the bottom end (c) so that it meets the top of the kite, like this:

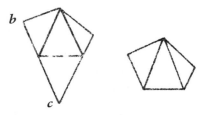

5. Now you have two points at the top (b). Fold one down toward you and the other away from you.

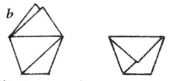

That's all! To use the cup, give it a little squeeze along the sharp sides. You'll find it opens up and is ready for action.

Warning: Not too much action. The cup may not last long. Don't fill it too full, and be watchful for leaks.

TABLE FOOTBALL

*Players: 2 (more can play in round robin tour-
    naments)*
Equipment: A sheet of paper
   *Table (ideal length for beginners is at least
   40 inches, or 1m, but you can play on a
   table of any length)*
   Any flat surface, such as a book or ruler
   Coin
*Preparation: Using the sheet of paper, make
   the football as shown below.*

Illus. 1

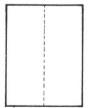

**Fold the sheet of
paper in half
lengthwise.**

**Then fold
it again
lengthwise.**

**Fold
over one
edge.**

And fold again and again as you would a flag.

Football

Tuck the edge into the football.

Flip a coin to see who goes first.

The first move: Set the football on end at the edge of the table as in Illustration 2.

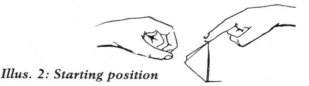

Illus. 2: Starting position

Or lay it flat—part on and part off the table—as shown in Illus. 3.

The first person to play

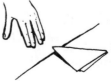

Illus. 3: Alternative starting position

then flicks the football with a finger or shoves it across the table. The object is to get the football *just exactly* on the edge of the opponent's side of the table, with one edge of the football sticking over the end of the table—*without going off.* This is a "touchdown" and it is worth six points.

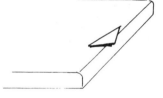

Illus. 4: Touchdown

Your opponent, without changing the position of the football, flicks it back with the same idea in mind.

The play continues, with players taking turns.

THE RULES

1. If you hit the ball off the table, you are charged with a "down." It is up to your opponent then to put the ball back in play, starting as in Illus. 2 or Illus. 3, from his or her end of the table.

2. When you have been charged with four "downs" of your own, you are "out" and your opponent gets a chance for a field goal (see Rule 6).

3. Touchdown: When you get a touchdown, it is worth six points and a try at an extra point. this "try" is a chance to make a field goal (see Rule 6).

4. You may not hit the football with your thumb or cover the football with your hand at any point during the game.

5. You may not pick up the football in the middle of play, unless you shoot it off the table, and are charged with a "down."

6. Field goal procedure: When you have been charged with three downs—before you are forced out—you can try for a field goal. You also get to try for one after you score a touchdown. For this you need to set up goal posts,

which are created by putting your fingers in
the position shown in Illus. 5.

Goal post   *Goal post*

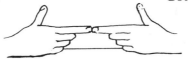

Illus. 5: Goal post position

Then the one doing the finger-kicking sets
up the ball on end (Illus. 2), approximately 3
inches (7.5cm) from the edge of the table,
and tries to send it above the bar and between
the goal posts.

To avoid arguments, the kicker is the one
to decide whether the kick is good or not.

A field goal is worth three points, unless it
takes place after a touchdown, in which case it
is worth only one extra point, just as in field
football.

After a field goal, the opponent starts the
ball back in play, beginning at his or her edge
of the table (Illus. 2 or Illus. 3).

PENNY SOCCER

Players: 2

Equipment: 3 or more coins
  (You can play with all pennies or any other
  group of coins. Playing with a variety of
  coins in the same game is more interesting.)

Preparation: None

You, sitting at one end of the table, are the
Defender. You place your index finger and
pinky on the edge of the table, with your
middle fingers bent underneath, like this:

Illus. 1

  The space between your fingers on the table
is the goal.

Your opponent—the Attacker—sits at the other end of the table, and arranges the pennies as in Illus. 2 or Illus. 3.

Illus. 2   *Illus. 3*

The first move: The Attacker—with four fingers bent—pushes or slip-pushes the pennies, just enough to break the formation and prepare for the next move.

IIllus. 4

The second move and all the moves after that are used to maneuver a penny into the Defender's goal. The Attacker may use any finger or fingers to shoot the penny through, but *not* his or her thumb. The Attacker gets as many turns as it takes (no one counts), as long as he or she doesn't break any rules.

THE RULES

1. The penny that the Attacker shoots must go in a path between the other two pennies.

2. The penny must not touch either one.

3. The penny may not go off the table.

4. To be a goal, the penny must hit your knuckles on the table edge.

5. If the Attacker has a difficult shot to make—a curve, for example—the player may use a pen or pencil to assist the shot. In Illus. 5 you see the problem the Attacker is up against.

Illus. 5

In Illus. 6 you see how a pen can be used to solve it.

Illus. 6

The players take turns trying to shoot a goal. If the Attacker breaks one of the rules, his or her turn is over and the Defender becomes the Attacker. The next time the opponent's turn comes up, the game begins all over again with the basic penny formation.

The player who makes the most goals, after an equal number of turns, wins.

PLAYING WITH MORE THAN THREE COINS

If you use more than three coins (you can use any number), begin with a pyramid formation like this:

Illus. 7

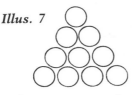

When you attack you must always designate the two coins you are shooting between. If your coin hits another coin on the table, your turn ends.

PENNY SOCCER FOR EXPERTS

Choose one of three pennies as the one you will shoot into the goal. Turn it heads up while the other two are tails up, or vice versa. If you score any other penny, your turn continues, but it does not count as a goal.

FLIP THE BOX

Players: 2 or more
Equipment: A matchbox
Preparation: If the matchbox has the same
    design on top and bottom, you'll need to
    mark it in some way so that you can tell
    which face is which. You can do that with a
    marker or a piece of tape.

Set the matchbox at the edge of the table, so
that about a third of it sticks out over the
table edge. Then, using your index finger, flick
it upwards.

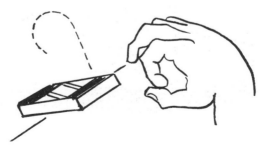

You can do this with your palm down or up, but always start the flick from your thumb and flick the bottom of the box.

Score 0 if the box lands top side down, 1 if it lands top up, 5 if it lands on its side, 10 if it lands on end.

You can play until it's time to stop, and then the one with the highest score wins. Or you can decide on the winning score before you start.

COOTIE

....

Players: 2 or more
Equipment: A sugar cube—or any other object
   with six equal sides
   Paper and pencil
   Cup
Preparation: On each side of the cube, write a
   letter:

   B (stands for Body)
   H (stands for Head)
   L (stands for Leg)
   E (stands for Eye)
   A (stands for Antenna)
   T (stands for Tail)

It's very sad that this game isn't played much anymore, but you don't find many restaurants these days that serve sugar cubes. And it isn't easy to find other objects with six sides. You can of course play it with dice, letting a number stand for each part. But how often do we carry around dice when we're traveling?

In any case, "Cootie" is a fun game and shouldn't be lost completely. It's similar to "Hangman" (page 194) in one way: you draw a creature, step by step, and when the drawing is completed, the game is over. But in "Hangman" you draw a person, and in "Cootie," you draw a flea.

A finished cootie looks like this:

In order to start your picture going, you roll the cube out of a cup onto the table. As soon as you roll a B (body), you can begin your drawing. This entitles you to another turn. But the next letter you come up with must be something that you can add to your picture. For example, if you throw an A for antenna, or an E for an eye, you haven't thrown a head yet. So you lose your turn. But, if you had thrown a head, a leg, or a tail, you could add any one of them easily, and you'd get another turn.

In order to complete your cootie, you need to throw:

1 Body
1 Head
6 Legs
2 Eyes
2 Antennae
1 Tail

First finished cootie wins and scores 13 points, one for each cootie part. Other players can total up the cootie parts they've drawn in order to come up with their score.

THE SIMPLEST SOLITAIRE GAME

Players: 1 or more
Equipment: A deck of playing cards
Preparation: None

This is one of the only card games it's possible to play successfully in a plane. You don't even need to have a tray table in order to play.

Turn over the cards, one at a time. As you turn them over, count aloud: Ace, Two, Three, Four, and so on—a word for every card. The object of the game is to get through the entire deck without ever having the word you say agree with the card you're turning over. If you should happen to be saying "Three," for example, while you're turning over a three, you have to stop, and your score is only the number of cards you've already turned up.

You can play five rounds of this game and tally up your score—or play against an opponent with whom you take turns.

241

THE SUGAR GAME

Players: 2 or more
Equipment: 3 packets of sugar or artificial
sweetener for every player, or you can use
pebbles or pieces of a drinking straw
Preparation: None

This terrific game is perfect for those times when you're waiting to be served at a restaurant. I've always suspected that the waiters didn't look too kindly on our family crushing and mutilating 12 of their sugar packets. But no one ever complained about it to us. As a matter of fact, I think many of them were interested in the game.

Each player puts none, one, two, or three of their packets into one fist, which is held out toward the other players. The other packets stay hidden in the other fist. When everyone is holding out a fist, the guessing starts. Each player guesses how many objects there are in total in all the fists being held out. Each one must guess a different number. Then, when the fists open up, the person who guessed right is the winner. One win scores one point. Highest number of points when the food comes, wins.

THE PENNY GAME

Players: 2 or more
Equipment: 5–10 pennies per player—or
   pebbles, pieces of drinking straw, or napkin
   scraps
Preparation: None

This game is similar to "The Sugar Game."
Your opponent holds out a fist with some of
the 10 pennies in it. Then you have to guess
whether the number of pennies is odd or
even. If you're right, you win a penny. If
you're not, you pay a penny. Then, it's your
turn to hold out a fist. The one with the most
pennies when the food comes wins.

8 The World's Most Challenging Games

IMAGINE THE FUN YOU'LL HAVE!

TEST

Why call these the world's most challenging games? Because they test our imagination as well as our skill at guessing and remembering and sensing things.

And once the imagination is at work, there's no limit to how interesting, complicated, surprising, and electrifying the play can be.

If you like to write, sketch, invent—or just experiment with ideas—investigate this section.

ESSENCES

Players: 2 or more
Equipment: None
Preparation: None

The most fascinating of all guessing games, "Essences" calls on your intuition, imagination, and logic—all at the same time.

Before the game begins, the players agree on what kind of subject will be used—whether it will be a famous person or a fictional character, or someone everyone knows (it could be someone who is present), which is the most fun.

Then one player thinks of a person and it's up to the others to identify him or her by finding out the "essence" of the person. There is no limit on the number of questions you can ask.

Here is a sample game:

BEN: I am thinking of a fictional character who is male. *(His subject is Ebeneezer Scrooge from Charles Dickens' A Christmas Carol.)*
DORIS: What music is this person?
BEN: Discordant modern music.
DALE: What animal is this person?
BEN: A skinny anteater.
MARJORIE: What color is this person?
BEN: Gray.
DORIS: What article of wearing apparel?
BEN: An old sweater. *(Ben resisted the impulse to say an old dressing gown, which is what is associated with Scrooge, but not what his essence is.)*
MARJORIE: What piece of furniture is this person?
BEN: An old Victorian bureau made out of dark wood with a marble top.
DALE: What tree?
BEN: An old gnarled oak with its leaves gone.

As you can see, no one can say whether your

answers are right or wrong, they are just your impression of what the character is like.

At some point in the questions, the guessers will want to summarize what they feel they know about the character you've described. At this point, you can set them more on the right track if you think you've led them astray with some of your answers. Generally, it's amazing how accurately they describe the person. And you're as delighted as they are when they get it right.

Other categories you can ask about:

restaurant	country
dog	book
fruit	sport
flower	car
mineral	food
house	time of day
dessert	movie

Even the driver can play this game.

PSYCHIC EXPERIMENTS

Players: 2
Equipment: A magazine with full-page illustrations
Preparation: None

Are you psychic? What better time to find out than when you're shut off from most distractions? This is a splendid game for bus, train, or plane, where all the usual preoccupations have been removed.

Open the magazine to an illustration, but keep the picture hidden from your partner. Then ask a specific question about it, such as, "How many people (or animals or houses or windows) are in the picture I'm looking at?"

Now concentrate as hard as you can on the people in the illustration while your partner tries to clear his or her mind and allow the picture to come through. The answer you get may be right or wrong, but in either case, go on to another question. Don't make a guessing game of it. If the answer is wrong, just say, "No, there are two people. Now I'm going to concentrate on what one of them is doing. Tell me what that is." And then go on to other questions.

The results may truly astound you. Researchers have found that people who think they are have psychic abilities are able to do far better in ESP experiments than people who think they haven't—or that telepathy doesn't exist. So the confidence you build up by getting an answer right can actually give much great strength to your psychic powers.

If you don't seem to be getting anywhere, change roles and let your partner choose the illustration and "send" the picture out to you. Sometimes it works better one way than the other.

MIND OVER MONEY

Players: 2
Equipment: A coin
  Paper and pencil or pen
Preparation: None

Can the mind influence inanimate objects and make them conform to its will? This is your chance to find out.

Take a coin. If you flip it a great many times, you should come out with an average of 50 heads and 50 tails in every 100 flips, according to the law of averages.

But suppose you have the power to influence the flip of the coin and cause it to turn up heads—or tails—a disproportionate number of times. Then you'd be upsetting the law of averages!

To try your powers, let one person concentrate on either heads or tails. The other keeps track of the number of tosses, and the number of times the coin turns up "right." Decide for yourself when you are the "influencer," whether you prefer to have the other person flip the coin, or whether you wish to flip it yourself and, perhaps, influence it more directly.

WRITING CHARADES

Players: 2 or more
Equipment: Pencil and paper
Preparation: None

You probably know how to play "Charades." You are assigned the title of a book, a song, a movie, a play—or you are given a proverb or a saying—and you act it out, word by word (sometimes syllable by syllable) so that your team can guess it in the shortest possible time.

"Writing Charades" is a little different. Instead of acting it out, you draw it. And the way you draw it can be very different from the way you'd act it out.

For example, *Cats* might be:

For example, *A Tale of Two Cities* might look like this:

"Little pitchers have big ears" might look like this:

"On Top of Old Smoky" might be:

Not all subjects are as easy to draw as those, however. You might get something like "I've Been Working on the Railroad," and if you don't get any bright ideas about how to put that idea across, you could choose to illustrate it word for word:

If just two of you are playing and there isn't anyone to assign a subject, you an each simply decide what you're going to draw. Then trade papers and figure them out.

If you're playing with more than three other people, you can form two teams. Each team thinks up a really tough subject, writes it down, and passes it along to a member of the opposing team. That person must draw the subject so clearly that the remaining team members can guess it fast. Both teams can play simultaneously, or go one at a time while the other team watches.

If you play this way, one team can time the other, limiting the number of minutes anyone can take to think up a subject, draw it, and guess it.

Speediest wins.

WORD ASSOCIATIONS

Players: 2
Equipment: None
Preparation: None

The first player names a noun. The second player has to answer with a word associated with it. For example, let's say the first player says "Cat." The second player (you) might say "Dog." Here the association is obvious—both are pets—and the answer gets you one point.

FUR!

BALL!

But what if you didn't say "Dog"? What if you said "Hat"? The first player might challenge you. And when you're challenged, you have to come up with a good reason why your answer is a valid choice. You might explain that you were thinking of Dr. Seuss's *The Cat in the Hat*, which would be a fine answer.

A successful challenger gets two points, while an unsuccessful challenger loses two points. So, if the first player did challenge you, he or she would end up with -2 (minus 2) points for that round. And, as a successful defender, you'd end up with +2. If you'd lost the challenge, you'd have lost two points also.

As you can see, an obvious answer is safe and will always get you one point. But a subtle answer, one that gets challenged but has a solid idea behind it, can put you 4 points ahead. It pays to be crafty!

If you're playing with more than two people, the third player would then go next with an association to the word "Hat." If only two were playing, the first player would go next with an association to "Hat."

Majority vote decides whether an answer is valid. If only two are playing, you can either work it out between you or let a third party decide.

MY GRANDMOTHER'S TRUNK

Players: 2 or more
Equipment: None
Preparation: None

Poor Grandma traveled with the strangest collection of stuff. Once she took a trip and in her trunk she carried fruit, feathers, foreign cars, fake jewelry, a fountain, and some other surprising objects.

On another trip her trunk contained pillows, parsley, portraits, penguins, a psychiatrist and, oddly enough, pajamas.

To play the game, the first player starts by mentioning one item that Grandma carried in her trunk. The next player repeats this item and adds another item that must start with the same letter.

Each time a new item is added, the player must repeat the whole list, starting with the first item, before adding on a new one, again an item starting with the same letter. The list must be said in the exact order it appeared originally. First person to make a mistake loses or is out of the game.

For a slightly more difficult game, don't start all Grandma's stuff with the same letter. Let her take anything she wants.

MY LADY'S LAPDOG

Players: 2 or more
Equipment: None
Preparation: None

This memory game may remind you of the song "The Twelve Days of Christmas," but instead of "A partridge in a pear tree," it keeps coming back to "My lady's lapdog."

The first player says, "My lady's lapdog."

The second player says, "Two ____-_____ and my lady's lapdog," filling in two of anything that begin with the same letter, such as two "fat fillies."

The next player adds three of something else, perhaps "three naughty novels," and goes on to repeat "Two fat fillies, and my lady's lapdog."

The fourth player might say, "Four happy hikers, three naughty novels, two fat fillies, and my lady's lapdog."

Keep the game going for as long as you like—or as long as you can—whichever comes first!

MY LADY'S LAPDOG—EXPERT'S GAME

Want a challenge? Instead of making the letters agree (fat fillies, naughty novels), choose completely unrelated words. A game might go like this:

ARLENE: My lady's lapdog.

DAVID: Two thoroughbred frogs and my lady's lapdog.

LEE: Three hungry elephants, two thorough bred frogs, and my lady's lapdog.

WAYNE: Four Egyptian pharaohs, three hungry elephants, two thoroughbred frogs, and my lady's lapdog.

And so on. It's much tougher!

269

STORYTELLING GAMES

Players: 2
Equipment: None
Preparation: None

This seems like other memory games at first glance. But instead of simply stringing ideas together, this intriguing game gets you telling a story. If you're interested in words or images or storytelling, and if the minds of the players are in sync, it can be a really creative and stimulating game.

In the simplest version of this game, the first player starts with a basic sentence—a sentence with no adjectives or phrases in it—something like "I am an actor" or "I went to Alaska." The sentence should have a noun in it that starts with A.

The second player repeats that sentence, but adds a phrase that contains the letter B. For example:

NICHOLAS: I am an actor....
TONI: I am an actor in Budapest....
PEGGY: I am an actor in Budapest playing comedies....

And so on, through the alphabet. Any player who cannot remember the story or continue it drops out.

Once two players have dropped out, they start their own game. The others, as they too drop out, join them. So the game continues until all are out except the winner. Then the winner joins the second game.

STORYTELLING IN MID-ALPHABET

In this variation on the game, you can start anywhere in the alphabet. For example:

LISA: I have a dream....
BRIAN: A dream of eternity....
PAT: I have a dream of eternity and freedom....
CANDICE: I have a dream of eternity and freedom among the ghosts of the past....

And so on. The only advantage to starting later in the alphabet is that you get a chance to use different letters than the usual A, B, C, and different words.

STORYTELLING IN FREE FORM

This is a little like the previous games, but here there are no restrictions—no restrictions on nouns or on letters or on anything else. You take turns building the story in any direction you want. For instance:

EVAN: I used to love to go sailing....

ELLEN *(can continue with another phrase or a whole new sentence):* I used to love to go sailing on a Chinese junk....

FRANCESCA: I used to love to go sailing on a Chinese junk until the fateful day when I met the magician....

GREG: I used to love to go sailing on a Chinese junk until the fateful day when I met the magician who practiced the black arts....

Getting interesting? Try finishing it yourself.

9 Lateral Thinking Puzzles

Puzzles are great to do alone, but it's a rare puzzle that you can do with other people and play like a game. Lateral thinking puzzles are just that. They are stories—very short stories—that leave out crucial information.

From the basic story itself, there's no way you can tell what is really happening—unless you break through your logical, step-by-step thinking and jump into imagination and creativity—or open yourself up to asking yes-or-no type questions that will reveal the facts.

The puzzles here each have clues, questions that the book answers, so that if you don't have anyone around to play with, you can play with this book. But if you do have people around—in a car, on a plane, train, or bus—you can be the one who poses the puzzle and answers their questions.

I first ran into these puzzles on a whale-watching ship, off the coast of Cape Cod. At the time, no whales were showing themselves. But a fellow on the boat had a group of people around him, all ages, all asking questions about a situation he had described to them, and he was answering yes or no. If there had been whales, I don't think that crowd would have noticed! They were having a great time. I was too.

So, take a look at these great puzzles. And

don't be shy about referring to the clues. They are an important part of the game. Once you have mastered these puzzles, try making up your own. It's tricky, but fun!

1. THE APPLE PROBLEM

There were six apples in a basket and six girls in the room. Each girl took one apple, yet one apple remained in the basket. How come?

Clues on page 291/Answer on page 344.

2. THE BOOK

A woman walked up to a man behind a counter and handed him a book. He looked at it and said, "That will be four dollars." She paid the man and then walked out without the book. He saw her leave without it but did not call her back. How come?

Clues on page 292/Answer on page 344.

3. A FISHY TALE

A woman had a pet goldfish which she loved very dearly. One day she noticed that it was swimming feebly in its bowl and it looked very unwell. She rushed to the vet with her prized pet and he told her to come back in an hour. When she returned, she found the goldfish swimming strongly and looking healthy again. How had the vet managed this?

Clues on page 293/Answer on page 345.

4. THE LOST PASSENGER
• •

Little Billy was four years old and both his
parents were dead. His guardian put him on a
train to send him to a new home in the
country. Billy could neither read nor write nor
remember the address, so a large label on a
string was secured around his neck clearly
indicating his name and destination. However,
despite the best efforts and kindness of the
railway staff, Billy never arrived at his new
home. Why?

Clues on page 294/Answer on page 345.

5. THE TRUCK DRIVER
• •

A police officer saw a truck driver clearly
going the wrong way down a one-way street,
but did not try to stop him. Why not?

Clues on page 295/Answer on page 345.

6. MOUNTAINS AHEAD

You are seated next to the pilot of a small plane at an altitude of one mile. Huge mountains loom directly ahead. The pilot does not change speed, direction, or elevation. How come?

Clues on page 296/Answer on page 345.

7. THE SEVEN-YEAR ITCH

While digging a garden, a woman unearthed a large metal box filled with money and jewelry. For seven years she spent none of the money and told no one what she had found. Then she suddenly bought a new house, a new car, and a fur coat. How come?

Clues on page 297/Answer on page 345.

8. THE FREE EXTENSION

A man went to a builder with plans for an extension to his house. They had never met before but the builder agreed to build the extension at no charge to the man. Why?

Clues on page 298/Answer on page 346.

9. HIGH OFFICE

Tom cannot read or write or tie his shoes. He has never worked a day in his life. Despite these shortcomings, Tom is given an extremely important, prestigious, and well-paid job. How come?

Clues on page 299/Answer on page 346.

10. MONEY TO BURN

A bank messenger, carrying a bag containing one thousand $100 bills, was robbed at gunpoint by a masked man. The man took the bag home and, without looking inside, burned it. Why?

Clues on page 300/Answer on page 346.

11. THE COWBOY'S FATE

Cowboys who lived in the Wild West led a dangerous existence. They were at risk from cattle stampedes, Indian attacks, rattlesnakes, disease, and gunfights. However, none of these was the usual cause of death, which was something routine but deadly. What was the most common cause of death among cowboys?

Clues on page 301/Answer on page 347.

12. BATH WATER

Some time ago, before central heating and water boilers, people would heat water on stoves. At that time a scullery maid was heating a large pan of water in order to add it to a bathtub that contained some water at room temperature. When the butler saw it, he told her off. "Don't you realize," he said, "that the longer you heat that water on the stove the colder the bath will be when you pour the hot water in?" He was right. Why?

Clues on page 302/Answer on page 347.

13. THE RANSOM

••

A rich man's son was kidnapped. The ransom
note told him to bring a valuable diamond to
a phone booth in the middle of a public park.
Plainclothes police officers surrounded the
park, intending to follow the criminal or his
messenger. The rich man arrived at the phone
booth and followed instructions, but the police
were powerless to prevent the diamond from
leaving the park and reaching the crafty villain.
What did he do?

Clues on page 303/Answer on page 347.

14. THE MOTORCYCLIST

••

A man is lying severely injured in the road.
He had quite deliberately stepped out from
the sidewalk in front of a motorcyclist who
had hit him. Why had the man done this?

Clues on page 304/Answer on page 348.

15. THE TWO VANS

In a bizarre accident, two identical vans simultaneously plunged over a dockside and into 30 feet of water. They both landed upright. Each van had a driver who was fit, uninjured by the fall, and conscious. One drowned but the other easily escaped. Why?

Clues on page 305/Answer on page 348.

16. THE DAMAGED CAR
••

A man was the proud owner of a beautiful
and expensive Mercedes sports car. One day
he drove it to an isolated parking area and
then smashed the window, scratched the
doors, and ripped out the radio. Why?

Clues on page 306/Answer on page 348.

17. THE WEATHER REPORT
••

A terse weather report once stated that the
temperature in a certain place at midnight on
June 1st was a certain number of degrees.
Where was the place?

Clues on page 307/Answer on page 349.

18. ODD ANIMALS

What do these animals have in common: koala bear, prairie dog, firefly, silkworm, jackrabbit, guinea pig?

Clues on page 308/Answer on page 349.

19. THE ELDER TWIN
....

One day Kerry celebrated her birthday. Two
days later, her older twin brother, Terry, celebrated his birthday. How come?

Clues on page 309/Answer on page 350.

20. HAND IN GLOVE
....

A French glove manufacturer received an
order for 5,000 pairs of expensive sealskin
gloves from a New York department store. He
then learned that there was a very expensive
tax on the import of sealskin gloves into the
United States. How did he (legitimately) get
the gloves into the country without paying
the import tax?

Clues on page 310/Answer on page 350.

CLUES FOR LATERAL THINKING MYSTERIES

●●

1. The Apple Problem

●●

Q Were any of the apples split or eaten?
A No.
Q Did each of the six girls get one apple?
A Yes.
Q Were there only six girls and no other
   people in the room?
A Yes.
Q Were there only six apples in the room both
   at the beginning and end of the process?
A Yes.
Q Did any girl get more than one apple?
A Yes.

2. The Book

Q Was he surprised that she left without the book?
A No.
Q Did she pay the money to buy the book?
A No.
Q When she gave him the money, did she receive something in return?
A No, not really, but she was quite happy to pay it.

3. A Fishy Tale

Q Did the vet change the water?
A No.
Q Did he give the fish any medication, food, or tonic?
A No.
Q Had the woman had the goldfish for a long time?
A Yes.

4. The Lost Passenger

Q Did someone deliberately harm or abduct
  Billy?
A No.
Q Was the label removed in some way?
A Yes.
Q Was Billy a little boy?
A No.
Q Did Billy destroy the name tag?
A Yes.

5. The Truck Driver

. . . .

Q Did the police officer and the truck driver
   both know that it was against the law to
   drive the wrong way down a one-way street?
A Yes.
Q Was there some emergency which justified
   either of their actions?
A No.
Q Should the policeman have taken action?
A No.
Q Was the truck driver committing a violation?
A No.

6. Mountains Ahead

Q Does the pilot have control of the aircraft throughout?
A Yes.
Q Is there a tunnel or hole or other way through the mountains?
A No.
Q Were you at any time in serious danger?
A No.
Q Did you fly over, around, or past the mountains?
A No.

7. The Seven-Year Itch

....

Q Did the woman wait in order to avoid
  observation by the police or criminals?
A No.
Q Was the money and jewelry stolen?
A Yes (but irrelevant).
Q Would she have liked to have spent the
  money earlier?
A Yes.
Q Was she in prison?
A No.

8. The Free Extension

Q Did the builder gain some benefit from this whole process?
A Yes.
Q Were the two men related or was there an existing business relationship between them?
A No.
Q Did the man subsequently provide some service, reward, or payment to the builder?
A No.
Q Was the man famous?
A Yes.

9. High Office

Q Was Tom chosen for a specific reason?
A Yes.
Q Does Tom have some particular skill or
  aptitude?
A No.
Q Could anyone be given his job?
A No.
Q Was the previous holder of the job able to
  read, write, etc.?
A Yes, he was very accomplished.

10. Money to Burn

••

Q Does this involve some kind of insurance
  claim?
A No.
Q Did the robber know what was in the bag?
A Yes.
Q Was the messenger part of the plot?
A No. He was honest.
Q Was the money genuine?
A No, it was counterfeit.

11. The Cowboy's Fate

Q Was this cause of death accidental?
A Yes.
Q Did it involve firearms?
A No.
Q Did it involve other people?
A No.
Q Did it involve animals?
A Yes.
Q Did these animals attack them?
A No.

12. Bath Water

Q Was the maid heating water on the stove
 in order to add all of it to the bath water?
A Yes.
Q Was the temperature in the house steady?
A Yes.
Q Was there anything unusual about the
 kitchen, the stove, the water, or the bathtub?
A No.
Q Was the water very hot?
A Yes, it was steaming.

SPLISH SPLASH!

13. The Ransom

Q Did the man receive a phone call at the phone booth?

A No.

Q Was the kidnapper in the park?

A No.

Q Did the kidnapper get the diamond safely out of the park?

A Yes.

Q Was any other person involved?

A No.

Q Did the diamond leave the park in some sort of vehicle or through a tunnel?

A No.

14. The Motorcyclist

Q Was the man trying to injure or kill himself?
A No.
Q Did he know the motorcyclist who hit him?
A No.
Q Did he expect the motorcyclist to stop?
A Yes.
Q Was the motorcyclist expecting the man to step out in front of him?
A No.
Q Did the man's profession have something to do with motorcycling?
A Yes.

15. The Two Vans

Q Can we consider the vans, their situations, and the fitness and skills of the drivers to be identical at the time of this accident?

A Yes.

Q Was one able to open a door and escape and the other not?

A Yes.

Q Did one of them do something different (and smarter) than the other?

A Yes.

Q If they had been driving cars rather than vans, would the outcome have been different?

A Yes. They would probably both have drowned.

16. The Damaged Car

Q Did he do this to make an insurance claim?
A No.
Q Did he deliberately and voluntarily damage his own car?
A Yes.
Q Was there a monetary reason for doing this?
A No.
Q Did he set out that day intending to damage his car?
A No.
Q Did something happen which caused him to damage his car?
A Yes.
Q Did he do it because he wanted to avoid some worse consequence?
A Yes.

17. The Weather Report

Q Is it possible to deduce where this is, from the information given?
A Yes.
Q Did the weather report give any other details?
A No.
Q Did the weather report state whether the temperature was in degrees Fahrenheit or Celsius?
A No.

18. Odd Animals

These animals all have something quite specific in common. However, it has nothing to do with habitat, foodstuffs, appearance, activity, procreation, zoos, or physical attributes. What is it?

19. The Elder Twin

Q Were Kerry and Terry genuine human twins, born of the same mother of the same pregnancy?
A Yes.
Q Was Terry, the older twin, born before Kerry?
A Yes.
Q Was her birthday always before his?
A Yes.
Q Does where the births took place matter?
A Yes.

20. Hand in Glove

Q Did the glove manufacturer smuggle the gloves into the country?
A No. He was a reputable businessman.
Q Did he disguise them as something else?
A No.
Q Did he pay *any* duty?
A No.
Q Are your goods impounded if you refuse to pay duty?
A Yes, the goods are then sold at auction to the highest bidder. (The value of the sets of gloves at auction would be higher than the duty.)

10 Quizzes

The quizzes are especially good to read aloud when you're with a group of people—like in the car, or in any other spot. They are fun, especially when several people are trying to come up with the right answers. You could figure, if you want, that each person would get 10 points for being the first one with the correct answer, making it a competition—or you could just read them aloud for everyone to guess, or you could read them silently and test yourself.

QUIZ #1 WHAT DID THEY HAVE IN COMMON?

1. What did Norma Jean Baker and Harlean Carpentier have in common?
a. They were both opera singers.
b. They were both political activists.
c. They were both Spanish dancers.
d. They were both movie "goddesses."

2. What did Archibald Leach and Marion Michael Morrison have in common?
a. They were both leading men.
b. They were both directors.
c. They were both writers.
d. They were both child stars.

3. What did Frances Gumm and Doris Kappelhoff have in common?
a. They were both animal activists.
b. They were both antique collectors.
c. They were both singers.
d. They were both circus performers.

4. What did Virginia McMath and Frederick Austerlitz have in common?
a. They were a dance team.
b. They were married to each other.
c. They owned a restaurant.
d. They collected stamps.

5. What did William Pratt and Laszlo Loewenstein have in common?
a. They were both tap dancers.
b. They were both bird watchers.
c. They played in musical extravaganzas.
d. They played in horror films.

6. What did Joseph Levitch and Dino Crocetti have in common?
a. A comedy act.
b. A dance team.
c. They were both mystics.
d. They both were crazy about Mexican food.

315

7. What did Nathan Birnbaum, Mendel Berlinger, and Melvin Kaminsky have in common?
a. They all spoke French fluently.
b. They were all comedians.
c. They all had great recipes for quiche.
d. They were all ballet dancers.

8. What did Margarita Carmen Cansino and Maria Magdalena von Losch have in common?
a. They were both weavers.
b. They were married to the same men.
c. They were both glamour queens.
d. They were both designers.

9. What did Reginald Kenneth Dwight, Henry John Deutschendorf, Jr., and Nathaniel Coles have in common?
a. They were all singers.
b. They were all flute players.
c. They all piloted their own planes.
d. They all were astronomy buffs.

317

10. What did Sean O'Feeney, Michael Igor Peschkowsky, and Allen Stewart Konigsberg have in common?

a. They were all blues singers.
b. They were all major film directors.
c. They were passionate chefs.
d. They were all jazz dancers.

Answers on pages 351.

ANIMATED FILM QUIZ #1

1. In the movie *Aladdin*, whose voice was used for the genie?
a. Robin Williams
b. Jonathan Winters
c. Sid Caesar
d. Robert de Niro

2. What kind of animal is Rasputin's sidekick in the animated film *Anastasia*?
a. fox
b. wolf
c. snake
d. bat

3. One of the songs in *The Aristocats* is "Everybody Wants to Be _____."
a. free
b. rich
c. a cat
d. a dog

4. The true calling of the pig in the film *Babe* is:

a. being a watchdog
b. feeding the chickens
c. wallowing in the mud
d. herding sheep

5. The skunk in the film *Bambi* is named:

a. Thumper
b. Flower
c. Beauty
d. Robert

6. The would-be witch in *Bedknobs and Broomsticks* was played by:

a. Angela Lansbury
b. Meg Ryan
c. Glenn Close
d. Meryl Streep

7. In *Charlotte's Web*, the spider Charlotte befriends a pig named:
a. Babe
b. William
c. Wilbur
d. Templeton

8. In *Fantasia*, what Disney character is the magician's assistant in "The Sorcerer's Apprentice" segment?
a. Donald Duck
b. Mickey Mouse
c. Minnie Mouse
d. Pluto

9. The only friends of Quasimodo in *The Hunchback of Notre Dame* are three:
a. gargoyles
b. orphans
c. bats
d. mice

10. Everyone makes fun of the big ears of the little elephant in *Dumbo* except his mother and his best friend, Timothy, who is a:

a. mouse
b. rat
c. chipmunk
d. duck

Answers on page 352

ANIMATED FILM QUIZ #2

1. *The Jungle Book*, the story of Mowgli, a boy who was raised as a wolf, was based on a book by:
a. Edgar Rice Burroughs
b. Wilbur Smith
c. Rudyard Kipling
d. Victor Hugo

2. *The Little Mermaid* was based on a story by:
a. The Brothers Grimm
b. Hans Christian Andersen
c. Hendrik Ibsen
d. Emanuel Swedenborg

3. One of Pocahontas's funny animal friends in the film *Pocahontas* is a:
a. squirrel
b. gopher
c. hummingbird
d. robin

4. *The Land Before Time* is about a baby dinosaur named Littlefoot who is a:
a. Tyrannosaurus Rex
b. Triceratops
c. Brontosaurus
d. Apatosaurus

5. All five of the songs in *The Lady and the Tramp* were co-written and some were also sung by the same person who did several of the voices in the film. That person was:
a. Dionne Warwick
b. Tina Turner
c. Rosemary Clooney
d. Peggy Lee

6. Simba, the young lion in *The Lion King*, gets great advice from Rafiki, a:
a. monkey
b. eagle
c. wildebeest
d. crow

7. *One Hundred and One Dalmatians* was based on a book by
a. Charles Dickens
b. Mark Twain
c. Dodie Smith
d. Judy Blume

8. In what animated film do a woodcutter and his son get swallowed by a giant whale named Monstro?
a. *Pinocchio*
b. *Jonah*
c. *Mulan*
d. *The Sword in the Stone*

9. The song "Whistle While You Work" came from what animated film?
a. *The Rescuers*
b. *Snow White and the Seven Dwarfs*
c. *Oliver & Company*
d. *Cinderella*

10. One of the outstanding characters in *Beauty and the Beast* was the French candelabra named Lumière, who sang "Be Our Guest." The voice of the Lumière belonged to:

a. Jerry Orbach
b. Yves Montand
c. Jean Marais
d. Roddy McDowall

Answers on page 352.

WEATHER QUIZ

1. In the Philippines they call it *baguio*, in the Indian Ocean they call it a *cyclone*. In the Pacific, it's a *typhoon*. What is it called in the northern hemisphere?
a. el niño
b. tornado
c. tropical storm
d. hurricane

2. It is estimated that lightning strikes the earth ___ times every second.
a. 10
b. 100
c. 1,000
d. 10,000

3. A *tsunami* is a:
a. tidal wave
b. monsoon
c. earthquake
d. volcano

4. "The north wind doth blow and we shall have snow." Is this true?

a. no
b. in the middle latitudes
c. always
d. only in arctic regions

5. What kind of weather can you expect when you see a ring around the moon?

a. rain or snow
b. strong winds
c. fog
d. thunderstorms

6. When are you most likely to see hail?

a. during tornados
b. in the winter
c. in a blizzard
d. during thunderstorms

7. A tropical storm becomes a hurricane when its wind speeds reach ____ per hour.
a. 62 miles (99km)
b. 50 miles (80km)
c. 74 miles (119km)
d. 85 miles (136km)

8. Tornadoes can exceed speeds of ____ per hour.
a. 75 miles (120km)
b. 100 miles (160km)
c. 300 miles (480km)
d. 450 miles (720km)

9. The great deserts of the world include the Sahara of Africa, the Gobi Desert of Asia, the Mojave, Great Basin, and Sonoran deserts of North America, and the Great Sandy Desert of:
a. India
b. China
c. South America
d. Australia

10. In order to see a rainbow, you have to be:
a. between the sun and the shower
b. outdoors
c. in the tropics
d. standing in the rain

Answers on page 352.

FESTIVALS AND HOLIDAYS QUIZ

1. The ninth month of the Muslim calendar, this holiday celebrates the day Allah sent the Koran—the Muslim holy book—to Mohammed. During this month, Muslims fast during the day and eat only at night. The month is known as
a. Ramadan
b. Muharram
c. Ashura
d. Shaban

2. Easter, commemorating the resurrection of Christ can fall anywhere from
a. March 22 to April 25
b. March 15 to April 15
c. March 25 to April 25
d. March 20 to April 20

3. For this Hindu festival, a New Year's celebration in India, 200 little clay lamps called Diwa lamps are lit and placed all over the house, which is spic and span and newly painted. Accounts are settled and new clothes are worn. It is called

a. Pongal
b. Holi
c. Diwali
d. Durga Puja

4. Little girls play a major role in the Doll Festival, celebrated on the third of March in Japan. Heirloom dolls are placed in rows on special shelves with offerings, and mothers and daughters visit each others' houses to look at them, play with them, and have a tea party. The day is also called

a. Apricot Festival
b. Peach Blossom Festival
c. Apple Blossom Festival
d. Cherry Blossom Festival

5. A holiday something like Halloween is celebrated in China on the first day of the tenth month. Masks are worn to represent ghosts and monsters, and then the "phantoms" are either helped with spells or driven out. The holiday is called

a. Hsia Yuan
b. Li Chum
c. Hs'in Nien
d. Tam Kung

SWEET 'N' SOUR PUMPKIN!

6. The birthday of Buddha, the great religious leader of the East, is celebrated on April 8th. In one country it is the custom to buy captive animals and set them free on that day in honor of the Buddha. What country is that?
a. Japan
b. China
c. Korea
d. Thailand

7. The Jewish Feast of Lights is celebrated for eight days, during which the story of the heroic Judas Maccabaeus is acted out. One candle in the candelabra called the Menorah is lighted each day, and each day the children get a present. The name of this holiday is
a. Passover
b. Succoth
c. Yom Kippur
d. Channukah

8. For the last century, the Mummer's Parade has ushered in the New Year in an American city. The word "Mummer" comes from a German word meaning "mask." The parade is made up of clowns and comics, groups in fancy dress, and string bands. The city it takes place in is

a. San Francisco
b. New Orleans
c. Philadelphia
d. Cleveland

9. Mardi Gras, the most famous carnival in the United States, takes place the week before Lent in New Orleans. It features a king and queen, a colorful parade, fantastic costumes, masked balls, pageantry, and much gaiety. How long has it been celebrated?
a. Since 1900.
b. Since 1760.
c. Since 1830.
d. Since 1898.

10. St. Catherine's Day was once an important celebration on November 25 in Quebec, Canada, but now it is mostly known for a delightful custom that was added about 300 years ago. That custom is:
a. a folk fair
b. a taffy-pull
c. trick or treating
d. cake-baking events

Answers on page 352.

Hink Pinks:
1. Large barge
2. Blimp chimp
3. Sick chick
4. Rat chat
5. Coarse horse
6. Glum chum
7. Grim swim
8. Neat beet
9. Sly fly
10. Dull gull

Hinky Pinkies:
1. Lucky ducky
2. Mighty nightie
3. Gruesome twosome
4. Flirty Gertie
5. Sicker ticker
6. Evil weevil
7. Pocket rocket
8. Chunky monkey
9. Kickin' chicken
10. Noodle doodle

ANSWERS TO LATERAL MYSTERY PUZZLES

....

1. The Apple Problem
The first five girls each took an apple. The sixth girl took the basket as well as the apple in it.

2. The Book
She was returning an overdue library book.

3. A Fishy Tale
The vet could see that the goldfish was dying of old age, so to spare the old lady's feelings he dashed out and bought a young but identical fish and disposed of the old one.

4. The Lost Passenger
Little Billy, as his name suggests, was a goat who unfortunately ate his label, so no one knew where he was supposed to go.

5. The Truck Driver
The truck driver was walking.

6. Mountains Ahead
The plane is sitting on the ground at the airport of Denver, Colorado.

7. The Seven-Year Itch
The woman had been shipwrecked. She found a pirate's treasure, but was not rescued for seven years.

8. The Free Extension
It is a true story and the man was Picasso. The builder wisely decided that by building the extension, he would be able to retain Picasso's rough sketch of the plans, which would be worth far more than the cost of the construction work. He was right.

9. High Office
Tom is an infant who is crown prince of his country. His father, the king, has just died leaving a very inexperienced new head of state.

10. Money to Burn
The robber's mother was a widow who owed the bank $100,000. The bank had threatened to repossess her house, so her son devised a plan. He forged $100,000 and she gave it to the bank messenger, who signed for it. The forgeries were good enough to fool the messenger, but would never have fooled the bank. So the son had to rob the messenger before he got back to the bank.

11. The Cowboy's Fate

The most common cause of death among cowboys was being dragged along by a galloping horse when the cowboy's foot was caught in a stirrup. This would occur during a fall or when mounting or dismounting.

12. Bath Water

The water in the pan was already boiling when the butler came in. The longer the maid now heated the water, the less of it there would be (because of the steam) to heat the tub and the water's temperature would not rise any further.

13. The Ransom

This is a true story from Taiwan. When the rich man reached the phone booth he found a carrier pigeon in a cage. It had a message attached telling the man to put the diamond in a small bag which was around the pigeon's neck and to release the bird. When the man did this, the police were powerless to follow the bird as it returned across the city to its owner.

14. The Motorcyclist
The man was an examiner testing a motorcyclist. He instructed the motorcyclist to go around the block and then to do an emergency stop when the examiner stepped out from the sidewalk. Unfortunately, another motorcyclist of similar appearance came by first. Knowing nothing of the arrangement, he hit the examiner.

15. The Two Vans
One man tried to open the front door of his van, but could not because of the water pressure. The other man climbed into the back of the van, easily opened the sliding door, and thereby escaped.

16. The Damaged Car
A few minutes earlier the man had been the driver in a fatal hit-and-run accident. He drove to the isolated area and made it look as though the car had been stolen and vandalized. He then phoned the police to report his car stolen. (This is a true incident. He was later caught and sent to prison.)

17. The Weather Report

Since the weather report did not specify degrees in Fahrenheit or Celsius/Centigrade, the temperature must have been the same in both scales. Only a temperature of –40 degrees is the same in both Fahrenheit and Celsius/Centigrade. That temperature for June would certainly make the place Antarctica.

18. Odd Animals

They are all imposters:
The koala bear is not a bear; it is a marsupial.
The prairie dog is not a dog; it is a rodent.
The firefly is not a fly; it is a beetle.
The silkworm is not a worm; it is a caterpillar.
The jackrabbit is not a rabbit; it is a hare.
The guinea pig is not a pig; it is a rodent (and it is not from Guinea, but from South America).

19. The Elder Twin

At the time she went into labor, the twins' mother was traveling from Guam to Hawaii. The older twin, Terry, was born on March 1st. Shortly afterwards, the mother crossed the International Date Line, and Kerry, the younger twin, was born. The date was February 28th. In leap years, the younger twin celebrates her birthday two days before the older twin, since February 28 is two days before March 1st.

20. Hand in Glove

The manufacturer sent 5,000 right-hand gloves to Miami and 5,000 left-hand gloves to New York. He refused to pay the duty on them, so both sets of gloves were impounded. Since nobody claimed them, both lots were subsequently sold off at auction. They went for a very low price (who wants 5,000 left-hand gloves?). Naturally, it was the clever Frenchman, who won with a very low bid at each auction.

WHAT DID THEY HAVE IN COMMON?

1. d: They were Marilyn Monroe and Jean Harlow.
2. a: They were Cary Grant and John Wayne.
3. c: They were Judy Garland and Doris Day.
4. a: They were Ginger Rogers and Fred Astaire.
5. d: They were Boris Karloff and Peter Lorre.
6. a: They were Jerry Lewis and Dean Martin.
7. b: They were George Burns, Milton Berle, and Mel Brooks.
8. c: They were Rita Hayworth and Marlene Dietrich.
9. a: They were Elton John, John Denver, and Nat King Cole.
10. b: They were John Ford, Mike Nichols, and Woody Allen.

ANIMATION FILM QUIZ #1

1. a; **2.** d; **3.** c; **4.** d; **5.** b; **6.** a; **7.** c; **8.** b; **9.** a; **10.** a

ANIMATION FILM QUIZ #2

1. c; **2.** b; **3.** c; **4.** c and d. *Littlefoot is known as a Brontosaurus in the film, but the true name of Brontosaurus is Apatosaurus;* **5.** d; **6.** a; **7.** c; **8.** a; **9.** b; **10.** a.

WEATHER QUIZ

1. d; **2.** b; **3.** a; **4.** b; **5.** a; **6.** d; **7.** c; **8.** c; **9.** d; **10.** a

FESTIVALS AND HOLIDAYS QUIZ

1. a; **2.** a; **3.** c; **4.** b; **5.** a; **6.** d; **7.** d; **8.** c; **9.** c; **10.** b

GUIDE TO THE
GAMES AND INDEX